GIRL STUFF

A Survival Guide to Growing Up

Margaret Blackstone
and
Elissa Haden Guest

WITH ILLUSTRATIONS BY
BARBARA POLLAK

Harcourt, Inc.

Orlando Austin New York San Diego Toronto London

For our mothers, with love

www.HarcourtBooks.com

Illustrations copyright © 2006, 2000 by Barbara Pollak

First hardcover and paperback editions 2000
Updated paperback edition 2006

The Library of Congress has cataloged the original editions as follows:
Blackstone, Margaret.
Girl stuff: a survival guide to growing up/written by
Margaret Blackstone and Elissa Haden Guest;
illustrated by Barbara Pollak.
p.   cm.
Includes bibliographical references and index.
Summary: A guide for girls explaining both the physical and psychological aspects of puberty.
1. Teenage girls—Growth—Juvenile literature.   2. Teenage girls—Physiology—Juvenile literature.
3. Puberty—Juvenile literature.   [1. Puberty.]   I. Guest, Elissa Haden.
II. Pollak, Barbara, ill.   III. Title.
RJ144.B53   2000
613'.04243–dc21   99-48021
ISBN-13: 978-0-15-201830-6 ISBN-10: 0-15-201830-1
ISBN-13: 978-0-15-205679-7 (pb) ISBN-10: 0-15-205679-3 (pb)

Text set in Fairfield
Designed by Lydia D'moch

EB 10 9 8 7
4500221132
Printed in the United States of America

Acknowledgments

We wish to thank:
Our science editor, Ivy Chen, community health educator for Planned Parenthood/Golden Gate, for so graciously and generously sharing her knowledge and experience; her suggestions, advice, and careful reading of the manuscript were invaluable. Dena Harris, M.D., and Erin D'Anna, C.P.N.P., for their thoughtful and expert reading. Paula Bard, M.A., M.F.C.C., and consultant, for her insights into the psychological and emotional development of teenage girls, and for sharing her experiences in fostering parent/child communication. Dr. Carol Zeits, consultant. Toni Guy, vice president of education, and Claire Sallee, community health educator, both for Planned Parenthood/Golden Gate, for their expertise and advice. Linda Lazier, Ph.D., director of Reaching More Girls Project, Girls Incorporated, for her time and help. Evelyn Robert, L.Ac., our consultant on alternative medicine. Sheila Smith, for her historical research. Cindy Navarro, R.N., for her inspiring mother/daughter puberty talk. Librarians Susan Faust and Helen Wiley. Sharon Dezurick and her fellow librarians at the San Francisco Public Library. Elaine Winter, principal, and Claire Copley, librarian, of The Little Red School House. Teachers Lisa Jeli, Erainya Neirro, Michelle Rounds, Bobby Ramos, and Natalie Stone of Presidio Hill School. The many principals, teachers, and students who kindly allowed us to observe their sex education classes. All the girls who helped us with this book, especially Gena, Katya, Anna, Sarah, Emily, Sarah, and Sarah and Kate Shaughnessy. Elizabeth Van Doren, our intrepid editor. Jean-Claude Comert, for his infinite wisdom. Phyllis Wender, our dear friend, agent, and mentor. We'd like to thank the amazing Jennifer Aziz; we couldn't have done the revised book without her. Thanks, too, to Lydia D'moch and Robin Cruise for their great work.

And we would like to thank each other, for more than twenty years of a rich and enduring friendship.

—M. L. B. and E. H. G.

More thanks:
My son, always. My brother, Neil Blackstone, who made it better. Trent Duffy, Felica de Chabris, Lucrezia Funghini R.N., Carla Seal-Wanner, Channa Taub, Rebecca Kinger, Clover Lalahzaer, Nick Malis, Pati Netto, Tom and Barbara Leopold, and, finally, the Skinner brothers, great men who guided me through my first pack trip in the Wyoming mountains, when I was twelve years old and just beginning to go through it all.

—M. L. B.

Molly, Jane, Bill, Denise, Sheila P., Jamie, Laura, Anna F., and my aunt Rowena. Special thanks to Mia and Louise, for all their advice and support. Paul B., for Palisades Amusement Park. Jo, Jane, Karen, Cis, Annie, and the late Claire N. and Cicely Y., for being aunts to me when I was growing up. My brothers, Chris, Nick, and Anthony. My dear old pals Kathy and Charlie. Jenny, my best friend for forty years. Cherry W., whose wisdom, love, and guidance in the past sustains me, always. I am grateful to my late father for being such a loving parent and for speaking so openly and sensibly about puberty and sex. Finally, I thank my husband and children, for each and every day.

—E. H. G.

Contents

Introduction

When we were kids there were certain words and phrases that made us cringe:

1. **Menstruation:** Sounded like a fatal disease.
2. **Pimples:** We had them—need we say more?
3. **Sanitary napkin:** The word *sanitary* next to *napkin* sounded positively revolting.
4. **Puberty:** Something wet and slimy, a creepy alien blob.
5. **Adolescent:** Sounded like a young criminal.
6. **"That time of the month":** As if suddenly you changed.
7. **Staining:** Ugh, and ugh to deal with.
8. **"How are you feeling?"** (in a parent's tone of voice): Ugh again.

When we were kids the *language* of puberty seemed to get in the way of understanding and accepting the whole wacky business of growing up. And of course it didn't help that we had to watch those embarrassing, weird black-and-white educational films at school. It was the 1960s and those films made growing up seem both antiseptic and alien.

Fortunately, things have changed. People have become a little bit more relaxed talking about puberty, the time in life when we change from a child into an adult.

The funny part, however, is that the language of puberty can still make kids cringe. Recently we asked some girls to give us their "cringe words," and here are some of their answers: *vagina, penis, stretch marks, breast, bra, puberty, rape, period, sex.*

Lots of girls mentioned the word *sex.* As one girl, Ali, age eleven, explained: "*Sex* is one of those words that if someone says it, you either crack up laughing or stare in disgust. I can't stand it! The worst part is your parents actually 'did it.'"

One thing we learned from talking and listening to girls was just how anxious they are about growing up. Change is rarely easy, often scary, and sometimes uncomfortable. This is partly why words like *puberty, bra,* and *sex* make us cringe.

And speaking of cringing, while it's true that life is full of embarrassing moments, it's full of wonderful and exciting ones, too.

Before we started writing *Girl Stuff,* we sent out questionnaires, interviewed girls, and spent many hours in sex education classrooms. We wanted to find out what girls wonder about, worry about, and look forward to in their teenage years.

In this book you'll find the facts about this crazy thing called puberty, and advice about how to cope with it. But you don't have to read this book all at once. It might be better not to. Puberty is a stage in life you'll want to adjust to step-by-step. Looking at the big picture too quickly and all at once can be overwhelming.

So, dip into this book when you want to, where you want to, and with whom you want to. You'll probably have some questions. And you may think you understand something only to realize six months later that you're not quite sure. That's natural. We are not supposed to get it all at once. Our brains don't work that way.

We hope you will find this book comforting and useful. But mostly we hope it will help you realize that you're not alone, that there's no such thing as a stupid question, and that nobody has all the answers. Growing up is a lifelong process. And there is always something new to learn.

One

What's Going On on the Outside

One of the weirdest words in the English language is *puberty*. Not only does it sound funny—*pew-berty* or *pube-hurty*—it also makes us feel funny now and then as we are going through it. Not ha-ha funny—although there is that, too—but scared, awkward, sad, wildly-happy-one-minute-and-utterly-miserable-the-next, gorgeous, ugly, kind, mean, goofy, silly, you-name-it funny.

Each of us experiences puberty differently. But one thing everyone would agree on is that puberty is a time of change and at least a certain amount of confusion. Okay, sometimes a *lot* of confusion. But given everything that is happening in your body, it's bound to be confusing. During puberty your

body changes from a child's body into an adult's body. Along with the physical changes, such as developing breasts and getting your period, come emotional changes. Later on we'll talk about how puberty affects our feelings, but right now let's take a look at why and *how* our bodies change.

HORMONES, YOUR GLANDS, AND CHANGES IN YOUR APPEARANCE

Did you know that before you notice any physical changes in your appearance, your hormones are already surging? *Hormones* are chemical messengers that travel through your bloodstream. Your hormones cause the changes that are about to happen, and like any good adviser, they begin to prepare you beforehand. So, just think, what you are starting to experience now, your body has actually been preparing for, for years.

How Long Does Puberty Take ?

The big changes can take place over three or four years. You can consider getting your period to be a big change. The development of your breasts is a big change, too. But it can take five to six years for all the little changes to occur. Girls usually begin puberty earlier than boys—and they *end* puberty sooner than boys, as well.

THE OUTSIDE FOR GIRLS AND BOYS

Girls and boys go through many of *the same* changes during puberty. They both:

- grow taller
- grow hair under their arms
- grow pubic hair
- get pimples
- get body odor
- experience mood swings
- experience romantic and sexy feelings

grow taller
romantic feelings
grow taller
mood swings
pimples
deeper voice
facial hair
wider shoulders
underarm hair
breasts
begin to menstruate
pubic hair
wider hips
produce sperm

The hormones that cause the changes you go through during puberty are called *sex hormones*. There are many different definitions of *sex*. In this case, we mean the two sexes, male and female. The female hormone *estrogen* is largely responsible for these changes in girls. And the male hormone *testosterone* is responsible for these changes in boys. Although we all have both of these hormones in our bodies, girls have more estrogen and boys have more testosterone.

Of course, girls and boys go through many *different* changes, as well:

Girls

* grow wider hips
* develop breasts
* develop more curves
* begin to release eggs
* get their periods
* have vaginal discharge

Boys

* grow wider shoulders
* grow facial hair and/or chest hair
* develop deeper voices
* produce sperm

The reason girls and boys go through different changes is because they have different *sex organs*. Both girls and boys have outer sex organs or genitals (which you can see) and inner sex organs (which you can't see).

Girls' outer sex organs are called the *vulva*. The vulva includes the:

clitoris
urethral opening
outer vaginal lips
inner vaginal lips
vagina
anus

- labia, or outer and inner lips
- clitoris, a very sensitive organ, a main source of sexual pleasure
- urethral opening, not a sex organ but the opening to where urine, or pee, comes out
- vaginal opening, or entrance, to the sex organs

7

Girls' inner sex organs include:

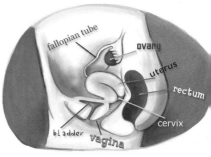

For a different view,
see page 63.

- two **ovaries,** which contain the eggs, or **ova** (when united with a male's sperm, an egg, or *ovum,* can develop into a baby)
- two **fallopian tubes,** through which the eggs travel from the ovaries toward the uterus
- the **uterus,** which catches the fertilized egg and houses the developing fetus as well
- the **cervix,** the neck of the uterus, with the opening that allows the sperm to meet the egg
- the **vagina,** the passageway between the internal organs and the outside of the body

Boys' outer sex organs include:

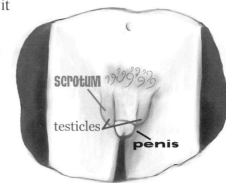

- the **penis,** an organ made of spongy tissue with blood vessels running through it
- two **testicles,** which hang in the scrotum behind the penis and produce the sperm that can fertilize an egg
- the **scrotum,** a skin sac that holds the testicles

Boys' inner sex organs include:

- two **epididymides,** a pair of long coiled ducts where sperm go to mature before they're released; these ducts carry sperm to the vas deferens

- the **vas deferens**, which carries the sperm cells to the urethra
- the **prostate gland**, the gland in which a whitish liquid is produced to help form semen—a combination of sperm cells and this whitish liquid

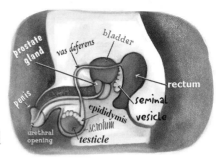

- the **seminal vesicles**, which also produce fluid that makes up semen
- the **urethra**, which carries semen through the penis and carries urine, too, *though not at the same time.*

circumcision

Circumcision is a surgical procedure that involves cutting away part or all of the **foreskin** (also called the **prepuce**) that covers the tip of the penis. Although its origin is not known, circumcision is a long-standing religious ritual in some populations, including among Jews and Muslims. The practice once served as a rite of passage for young

males at the onset of puberty, but today it is most often performed on newborn baby boys. Some people argue that circumcision makes it easier to clean the penis, while others say there are no proven health benefits. Circumcision is, ultimately, a purely personal choice made within the context of each family.

How Many Holes Do We Have Below the Waist?

Our friend Ivy is a health educator who often asks her students: "How many holes do you have below the waist?" The answers are: Boys have *two:* the *anus* (where feces, or poop, comes out) and the *urethral opening* (where urine, or pee—and, *at separate times, semen,* which carries sperm—comes out). Girls have *three* holes: the anus, the urethra, and the *vagina.* Females have this "middle hole" because our peeing and our sexual and baby-making functions are separate.

What comes out of the vagina? A regular vaginal discharge. Blood and tissue from a girl's period comes out of her vagina and, if she has one, one day, also a baby.

Why Are My Feet So Big?

Okay, you're saying to yourself, *"My feet are already bigger than my mother's. Soon they will be bigger than my father's feet!"*

If it's any comfort, humans are a bit like puppies—their feet grow first. They do this to provide stable platforms to support our growing bodies. So, one of the first signs that puberty is starting is your increasing shoe size. (Of course, when it comes to changes in your body, nothing is predictable. Your best friend's feet may grow faster than yours, and your breasts may start to grow before hers.) But your feet do stop growing even before you have reached your adult height. So, don't worry. They may start growing first, but they stop growing first, too. You just have to trust that your body knows what it's doing.

If you are really worried about the size of your feet, wear dark shoes and dark socks, not light.

BREASTS

Another early sign of puberty is the beginning development of breasts. The first change you see when your breasts start to develop is called *breast budding*. You'll notice that your nipples stand out a little farther from your chest. You may also feel something like a hard lump behind the nipple. Often one breast begins to develop before the other. In fact, one breast may end up being a little larger than the other. Sometimes the nipples feel sore and tender or even itchy. *This is normal.*

I Thought Buds Are Flowers ?

You're absolutely right. Buds *are* baby flowers, the first step toward the blooming of a rose, a tulip, or almost any of your favorites. Your *breast buds* are the first stage in the development of your breasts.

Of course, they probably don't seem like buds to you. After all, they're part of your body, and they're changing right before your eyes. This may seem a little surprising, as what were once just nipples begin to bulge slightly from your chest. Some girls feel embarrassed when they start to "develop"; others feel proud. Both reactions are normal. The best thing to do is to try to accept the new way you are starting to look, because it's nature's way—and there's nothing you can do about it, anyway.

Did You Know?

Did you know that, except for the first year of your life, the year after breast buds appear is the year in which you grow the most? You'll add more inches to your height—and often your feet, too—in that year than in any other year of your life.

Why Do We Have Breasts?

Females develop breasts (also known as *mammary glands*) so they can nurse their young.

When a woman gives birth, it is the job of the breasts to make milk for her baby. A woman doesn't have to breast-feed her baby, but if she chooses to, the glands in her breast are ready to produce milk. The size of a woman's breasts has nothing to do with how much milk she produces. Big and small breasts have the same number of milk glands.

Why a Bra?

There is no rule that says every girl or woman must wear a bra. It's really a matter of comfort and choice. Some girls prefer to wear undershirts or camisoles. Others prefer to wear bras. Some wear bras some of the time, and undershirts or camisoles other times. And still other girls choose to wear nothing to cover or support their breasts.

What Size Bra?

You can either measure yourself at home or a saleswoman can measure you in the privacy of a dressing room.

If you decide to measure yourself at home, take a tape measure and measure around your chest just under your breasts. Add five inches to the number you get and round up to the next even number. Bras come in the following sizes, based on chest measurements in inches: 28, 30, 32, 34, 36, 38, and to the mid-40s. The letters on a bra size refer to the cup size of the bra, and range from *AAA* to *EE*. The *A*s and *B*s are for smaller breasts, and the *C*s, *D*s, and *E*s are for bigger breasts.

Once you know how many inches you measure around your chest, you can pick out different cup sizes to see which one fits best. When the bra is fastened, the cups shouldn't pucker or wrinkle. Puckering means the bra is too big. If your breasts stick out on the side or the bra cuts into you, it's too small. A bra that is just right should be smooth across the cups and fit snugly but not too tight across your back.

If you're having trouble or feeling frustrated trying to find the right fit, ask for help. Saleswomen know how a bra should fit. If you feel embarrassed, it might help to remember that they went through this, too.

If your breasts are tender when you run around, or if they feel heavy, you'll probably feel more comfortable wearing a bra. The most important thing to know about buying a bra is: *Go for comfort.* You wear a bra right next to your skin, so you'll want something that feels soft and isn't scratchy or too tight. You might try a bra made of pure cotton.

Department stores usually have a wide selection of bras. Try on different brands and styles to see which one fits the best. (Just as you may have noticed that a certain style of sneaker fits your foot better than others, it's the same deal with bras.)

HAIR, HAIR EVERYWHERE

Yet another of the changes in your body's appearance that may occur before your first period is the appearance of sparse *pubic hair*. (The *pubis* is the triangular area between your legs.) Pubic hair appears around the vulva, between your legs, and is usually similar in color to the hair on your head. It's perfectly normal, however, if your pubic hair is a different color from the hair on your head. As time goes by, the pubic hair will thicken and sometimes darken, if initially it was light in color.

Body Hair

During puberty you will also notice hair growing in your armpits and on your arms and legs.

You may also notice new hair on your face, in the mustache and sideburns areas.

As far as *body hair* goes, some girls have more and some have less. Some body hair is light and some may be very dark. This all depends on your hair color, how much body hair your parents have, and your ethnicity.

Some people find body hair attractive. Some don't. How we view body hair depends a lot on our own culture and family. If somewhere down the road you decide you want to shave, bleach, or remove body hair, it's *very important* for safety reasons that you talk to your mother or an older sister or friend about how to go about it.

16

SHAVING

Shaving is the cheapest and most convenient way to remove unwanted body hair. But you have to do it regularly. How often depends on the thickness and darkness of your body hair. If you have a lot of hair, you will have to shave more often than girls who have less hair do. Some say that shaving makes hair grow in faster and thicker. And shaving delicate areas like the bikini line can cause a rash.

Shaving is the easiest and least painful way to remove underarm hair and leg hair. It's best to buy your own razor (don't use your mom's, dad's, brother's, or sister's without asking), and make sure you change the blade often—a dull blade can cause cuts or rashes. But remember: Razor blades are sharp. So take your time. Shave against the direction of hair growth (i.e., when you shave your legs, shave up, not down). And try shaving with shaving cream instead of soap. It makes shaving much easier.

Shaving is *not* a good idea when it comes to your face; it will leave you with noticeable stubble and may make hair grow back thicker and darker. There are much better ways to tend to facial hair.

TWEEZING To tweeze, or pluck, a hair, you simply hold the tweezers in one hand, clamp down on the base of the unwanted hair, and pull it out quickly. *Tweezing* is not a good idea if you have more than a few unwanted hairs. Repeated tweezing can damage the hair follicle itself, making it harder to remove the hair in the future.

WAXING *Waxing* is very effective for hair removal from legs and for making hair stay gone longer than shaving. But it can be expensive and a bit painful, kind of like pulling off giant Band-Aids. Discuss this choice with your mother or another adult. You want to find a waxer who is experienced, gentle, and quick, and who works in a well-established hygienic facility.

When you get your legs waxed, it will be done in a private room. The people who do waxing have seen *everything*, so don't feel uncomfortable. Usually you lie down on a table. The waxer spreads warm melted wax on your legs and then applies strips of cotton cloth, quickly pulling off the wax along with the hair.

In addition to waxing their legs, people also get their underarms, bikini lines, and facial hair waxed. But since waxing might make your skin temporarily red and blotchy, it's a good idea to give yourself a day in between waxing and any public event you're planning to attend.

DEPILATORIES
Depilatories are chemical hair removers. They are convenient and, like shaving, using a depilatory allows you to remove hair in the privacy of your own bathroom. But some depilatories contain very harsh chemicals. If you have sensitive skin, you may remove unwanted hair but end up with an unwanted rash!

There are many depilatories on the market. You can buy a cream, lotion, or foam formula, depending on which you like best. It is a good idea to talk to your doctor or pharmacist before deciding on one. And be sure to choose one specifically formulated for the area—legs, bikini line, or face—that you want to remove hair from. After using a depilatory, use a moisturizer to prevent skin irritation or the formation of a rash.

BLEACHING
Bleaching is probably not appropriate for lightening leg hair if you have a lot of it. Bleaching, however, can be perfect for a slightly heavy mustache, if you are not interested in or willing to try waxing or electrolysis. But  don't forget that bleaches, like depilatories, contain harsh chemicals and can cause rashes. They need to be kept far away from your eyes. And again, it's a good idea to talk to a parent or a pharmacist *before* you use any product like this.

Flash! If you are African American or a girl who has dark skin, you should not use bleach on your skin. It can cause your skin to lighten when you don't want it to, because it bleaches your skin along with your hair.

ELECTROLYSIS

Electrolysis is a way to eventually remove hair permanently. Most women who choose electrolysis do so just for facial hair. This is how it works: With tools powered by electricity, the technician removes the hair at the base of the hair follicle, which prevents it from growing back. Electrolysis is expensive and some people say it's painful. Still, many women find that the earlier you start, the less electrolysis hurts and the more effective the treatment.

LASER HAIR REMOVAL

Laser hair removal is the newest and, many believe, most effective form of hair removal. But it is not a procedure to use on hair as fine as peach fuzz. This technique should only be used for the removal of coarse, dark unwanted hair.

Does laser hair removal hurt? Well, yes, but not very much. People describe the sensation as a quick pinprick, somewhat similar to the sensation you get when removing a Band-Aid or plucking a hair with a tweezers. Remember, though, if you're having a large amount of hair removed, you'll experience many pricking sensations. The biggest drawback of laser hair removal is that it is expensive.

BODY ODOR

During puberty we begin to sweat more (hormones at work again!), and sometimes sweat can make us smell. This smell is called *body odor,* better known as BO. Some kids notice more body odor, some notice less.

There is nothing wrong with body odor. It is perfectly natural. But some people are embarrassed by it and want to control it. Washing regularly with soap and water (especially after exercising) is an excellent way to minimize body odor.

If you notice that washing with soap and water isn't doing the trick, and you're not happy with the way you smell, try deodorant. Tell your mother, father, or an older sister, brother, or friend you need deodorant, or just go ahead and buy it.

Two products are often lumped together under the heading of deodorants—deodorants and antiperspirants. The difference between the two is simple: A *deodorant* works to control body odor, but it does not stop you from sweating. An *antiperspirant,* on the other hand, actually works to reduce the production of sweat. This makes an antiperspirant very effective in controlling body odor, because it is the bacteria in your sweat that causes body odor. The drawback is that it's healthy to sweat, and it is probably not such a good idea to interfere with the body's natural functions. Check the label before buying any deodorant product to see if it contains an antiperspirant. Unless you sweat very heavily, a deodorant alone will probably meet your needs.

There are many deodorant products on the market—so many, you could go bug-eyed looking for one. You might find out what your mother or friends use, or ask the people at the drugstore for advice. You might want to try one for sensitive skin, or an unscented one, first. You can also buy natural deodorants in almost any drugstore or natural foods store. A *natural* deodorant doesn't contain any chemicals or aluminum. Some people use a "baby powder" made of cornstarch instead of deodorant.

If you have developed a lot of underarm hair, it can contribute to body odor because the hair can trap moisture and cause more sweating. You may want to consider shaving regularly to avoid adding to body odor.

Why Do Humans Sweat?

Sweating is the way we cool down our body temperature. Dogs pant, humans sweat.

GAINING WEIGHT

Weight gain during the preteen and teenage years is normal, natural, and healthy. In fact, in order to get your period, you need to have about 20 percent body fat. Remember, this is the time that your body is developing into a *woman's* body. And a woman's body is *supposed* to be bigger than a girl's body. You can expect to gain anywhere from ten to thirty pounds or more during puberty, depending on your body type. Don't worry about it; your body knows what it's doing. Once again, it's important to remember that how and when *your* body changes will be different from how every other girl changes, and as individual as you are.

You might notice that during puberty your hips begin to widen. There's a good reason for this. Your hips aren't just hips, they're what frame your uterus and other internal organs. Your hips widen to provide more room in which a baby may grow, should you choose to have a baby one day.

Some girls are thrilled with their new womanly figure. Others are uncomfortable and self-conscious. It takes time for most of us to adjust to changes.

The Curse of the Scale

Let's face it, the weight thing haunts us all—girls and women. Our culture tells us, from a very early age, we will be happier and more successful if we're thin. This is not only silly, it's also not true. And it puts a terrible pressure on us. This pressure is especially hard to take during puberty, when your body is doing what nature needs it to be doing—gaining weight.

One way to lift the curse of the scale is not to own one. Even if others in your family insist on having a scale, you certainly don't need to weigh yourself on a daily, or even a weekly, basis. The less you worry about your weight, the happier you'll be.

The most important thing to remember is that nobody, but *no*body, is perfectly and completely comfortable with her body. Everybody worries about something. The key is not to let occasional worries take over your life.

If you find that you're thinking all the time about what you eat and how much you weigh, talk to your parents or another adult you trust. You might also consider seeing a counselor. There are lots of good advisers who can help you not to worry so much.

UNSAFE SECRETS

Sometimes it's unsafe to keep a secret. If you know or suspect a friend has an eating disorder, as hard as it may be, you must tell a parent or some other trusted adult right away.

Eating Disorders

Eating disorders are physical illnesses, but they often are caused by emotional issues. It's no accident that in a culture obsessed with dieting, weight, and appearance, eating disorders are very common.

Young girls are especially prone to eating disorders, for many reasons. Growing up is a time full of pressures. Most of us feel the pressure to be accepted and to do well at everything from school studies to sports to looking the best we can. And just as we are feeling the pressures of growing up, we are being inundated with information about the "right" way to look and, most of all, about being thin. Almost daily we see pictures of skinny people, pictures of food, food, food, and articles about new fad diets or drugs to help us lose weight. We can't get away from the subject of what we eat and how we look.

What may start as an innocent diet to lose a few pounds can turn into a diet curse. A girl may find herself unable to stop thinking about food; she may move food around her plate without eating a bite, hide food in odd places, or cause herself to throw up. She may tell people nothing is wrong when she's really tearing herself up inside, trying to deal with this monster of a problem. If you notice a friend behaving this way or you find yourself thinking, *Wow! That sounds like me,* you've got to talk with a grown-up you trust and get help. As hard as it is to ask for help, *you must* because eating disorders can damage your health and even threaten your life. The good news: You *can* get help and you *can* recover.

ANOREXIA   *Anorexia nervosa* is an eating disorder that affects many girls. Girls who are anorectic starve themselves to lose weight. They tend to be extremely skinny but still believe they're fat. They also tend to be afraid of, or even repulsed by, their developing bodies. Girls who are anorectic may get hungry, but they force themselves not to eat in order to keep losing weight. It may be scary to think about, but it's important to realize that anorexia is extremely dangerous.

Anorexia usually affects girls between the ages of thirteen to twenty-five, but it can affect girls as young as seven. Anorexics may stop getting their monthly periods. They may also be bulimic (see below).

If you find yourself resisting food even when you are literally starving, weighing yourself over and over again, or exercising compulsively, you should talk to an adult you trust about what could be a serious problem. With help, anorexia can be successfully treated.

BULIMIA   *Bulimia* is an eating disorder that involves extreme overeating and then periods of extreme dieting. There are two types of bulimia, purging and nonpurging. Purging involves eating large quantities of food, then vomiting the food and/or abusing laxatives. Nonpurging bulimia involves eating large quantities of food and then fasting and/or over-exercising to avoid weight gain. Bulimia is as dangerous to your health as anorexia.

Girls who are bulimic may be of normal weight or even a little bit overweight. They're just as obsessed by and terrified of food as anorexics, but they tend to binge and then diet. *Bingeing* means consuming a huge amount of food—thousands of calories—at one time and then intentionally getting rid of the food by throwing up or having diarrhea. Bulimics may also be anorectic.

Bulimia usually begins later in the teenage years but can begin at a younger age. Girls who are bulimic tend to be aware they have an eating problem but are unable to control it. If this describes you, take a deep breath and talk to a grown-up about getting help. Bulimia is treatable, and girls generally make an excellent recovery.

GETTING HELP It makes sense that beginning to eat normally is one of the first things girls with anorexia or bulimia are encouraged to do. This isn't all that easy and sometimes takes months, even years, to accomplish. But it's most important to remember that there are emotional problems that accompany the physical ones. Many anorexics also suffer from serious depression, and bulimics are typically troubled by severe emotional problems, as well. Thus, talking through the problems with a counselor or therapist is as important as learning to eat well again.

THE BODY WONDERFUL

When we're little, we're comfortable with our bodies. We run, leap, climb, swing from ring to ring, hang upside down, jump rope, bounce balls, and spin round and round. We know what a great feeling it is to run, full speed ahead, heart thumping, legs pumping. We don't question how wonderful our bodies are—we *know* they're wonderful.

And then we enter puberty. Many of us become overly critical of ourselves. Sometimes we judge ourselves so harshly that we are unable to see our good points at all. We may worry so much about how we look that we lose sight of who we are and all that we are capable of.

If you find you're feeling low about your appearance, talk to the women you know about how they dealt with these feelings. They've all been there. And they've found ways to feel comfortable with themselves and to find a "look" that's right for them.

Here are some suggestions for how to feel better about yourself:

* Don't compare yourself to others. This is a habit we all need to break. There are little steps you can take toward this end. For example, if you find that looking at fashion magazines makes you feel insecure, *stop reading the magazines.* If you find yourself thinking, *My best friend has such pretty hair and mine is ugly,* don't dwell on this thought. Instead, redirect your attention to something positive. If you're in a lousy mood and you can't find anything positive about yourself—or about anything else, for that matter—then try distracting yourself. Listen to music, curl up with a good book, go for a walk, watch a funny video.

* Don't criticize someone else's appearance to her face or behind her back. Everybody is sensitive about her looks, and personal remarks are rude and very hurtful. If a bunch of kids are talking about "feeling fat" or about how

so-and-so is "fat," try to change the conversation—or at least don't join in. Criticizing ourselves and others is not good for anyone. Doing so makes everybody more self-conscious and insecure.

✽ Find a physical activity that you enjoy. People who exercise feel better about themselves.

✽ Get involved with activities that have to do with your mind, such as reading, debating, drawing, or playing an instrument.

✽ Check out the website www.mind onthemedia.org, and join other girls who are involved with changing the media's beauty standards. This might give you a whole new perspective. You'll see you're not alone—women have been struggling with beauty issues for centuries!

✽ Get involved with your community, a fine way to see how important your contributions can be.

The more involved you are with life—and the less involved you are with how you look—the happier you'll be.

Beauty and the Brainwash

It's hard to feel positive about how we look if almost all we see in magazines and commercials are tall, thin models. Remember, if you look in the mirror and go, "*Yuck!*" that's society doing your thinking for you. Write to the magazines and tell them you're tired of seeing skinny models. Tell them you want to see real girls with real bodies.

Before

What Do MODELS Really Look Like?

After

(or, Oh, What a Little Technology Can Do!)

Did you know that computer programs make it possible to erase a model's pimples or scars? They can also change the shape of her eyes, cheekbones, breasts, and figure. More often than not, when we see a model's photograph, her real looks have been changed and "perfected." The woman we long to look like doesn't exist!

Makeup Tips
from Ancient Times

People have been preoccupied, for ages, with their looks and how to improve them. The ancient Egyptians were big on eye makeup. To the ancient Chinese, long red nails were a sign of beauty. Wealthy women in fifteenth-century France wore powdered wigs to cover their lice-ridden hair. In the late 1800s some American women applied a paste of the poison arsenic to their faces to get rid of pimples. They ate chalk to whiten their complexions. They used a recipe of sour milk and horseradish to remove freckles. To make their figures look attractive and fashionable, women wore corsets so tight that some of them ended up dislocating, or moving, their internal organs!

Thousands of years ago women used henna for skin and hair dyes, ochre for rouge, kohl for eye makeup, and pumice as a tooth whitener. They wore earrings made from emeralds and rubies. They wore hairpins of gold and silver, turquoise and jade. They painted their skin. They braided their hair.

France big hair 18th century

corset late 1700s

bullet bra 1950s U.S.

normal bound feet - China

Some Things Never Change

Today women still use henna, they still whiten their teeth, line their eyes, rouge their cheeks, and lighten their skin with powder or darken it with tanning lotion. They still wear earrings made from gems and semiprecious stones. They still wear hairpins. And they still braid their hair.

A Healthy Body and a Healthy Mind

It sounds corny and everyone's already told you, but it's still true that eating good food in the right amounts is not only good for you but will make you feel better, too. Your growing body needs adequate sleep, plenty of exercise, and a great deal of good food every day. The average teenage girl needs to consume approximately 2,200 calories a day, and if she's involved in sports, she may need an additional 600 calories or more per day. So, you have a lot of calories to play with. You can eat well, enjoy what you eat, have food treats, too—and still stay in shape.

Food as Fuel

Unfortunately, we live in a fast-food culture. We don't take enough time to enjoy our meals, and gulping down our food can lead to indigestion. Many of us skip meals altogether and then grab something junky to eat.

If you don't have enough time to relax over your breakfast or lunch, at least try to eat something that's good for you—that will give you energy. Four to six healthful snacks during the day can work as well for you as three big meals daily. You can graze—and as long as you're grazing on good food, you'll be fine.

A Short List of Nutrition Tips

🍴 *Try to stay away from processed food.*

🍴 Stick to fresh fruits, like peaches, apples, strawberries, bananas, plums, apricots, and melons. They're delicious and good for you.

🍴 Eat plenty of raw vegetables, plain or with tasty dips, such as guacamole, hummus, and black bean.

🍴 Snack on almonds. They're high in protein, and they have fewer calories than most other nuts.

🍴 Eat mostly whole-grain breads, crackers, and cereals.

🍴 Snack on matzos, crackers, breadsticks (made without hydrogenated oils) instead of potato or corn chips.

🍴 Eat protein—you need it. Eggs, cheese, chicken, fish, and lean beef are all good choices, as well as tofu and nuts.

🍴 Try all-natural yogurts with live acidophilus cultures for a great dessert or topping.

🍴 Choose cereal with milk and fresh fruit as a wholesome, well-rounded snack or meal any time of the day.

🍴 Limit how much saturated fat you eat, particularly in junk food.

🍴 Drink water instead of soda. Water is good for your digestion, *and it's good for your skin!*

🍴 *Don't starve yourself!* Doing so will only hurt you in the end and waste your positive energy on a hopeless, unhealthy project.

How we look at what we eat has changed for the better over the past several decades. We now understand that complex carbohydrates—fruits, vegetables, nuts, grains, and beans—are very important to our overall health, and we also understand that adequate amounts of protein are equally important. In addition, some new research has proven that foods high in fiber—whole-grain breads, most fruits and vegetables, and beans—also help to keep the body healthy. Here are some tips for a healthy diet.

- ♈ *Breads, cereals, and other complex carbohydrates: 6 to 11 servings per day.*
- ♈ *Vegetables: 3 to 5 servings per day*
- ♈ *Fruits: 2 to 4 servings per day*
- ♈ *Dairy products (milk, yogurt, and cheeses): 2 to 3 servings per day*
- ♈ *Meat, poultry, fish, nuts, dry beans, eggs: 2 to 3 servings per day*
- ♈ *For fats, oils, and sweets: The news is as to be expected—use them sparingly.*

Research shows that some unsaturated fats are very good for you, chief among them omega-3 fatty acids. So don't say no to fats completely; just bone up on your nutrition facts so you choose the right ones—in other words, skip the lard and use olive oil instead.

A Guide for Vegetarians

A number of growing girls are becoming vegetarians. A vegetarian diet is very healthful as long as it includes enough protein and iron. (Good sources include tofu, beans, nuts, cheese, and other dairy products.) Before you try these vegetarian snacks and meals, it's a good idea to consult with your pediatrician to make sure your diet is healthy and balanced.

- Enjoy anything from the foods on page 34 that don't include meat.
- Eat nuts, particularly almonds and walnuts.
- Choose whole-grain crackers and breads, and add a piece of cheese.
- Enjoy yogurts with live acidophilus cultures.
- Snack on raw vegetables—such as asparagus, broccoli, cauliflower, green beans, and zucchini—with dips.
- Have fruits with high-fiber content, such as apples, apricots, bananas, grapefruits, peaches, pears, plums, strawberries, and tangerines.
- Try bean dip and tortilla chips.

Exercise and Your Changing Body

When we're young we may take our bodies for granted, particularly those of us who aren't athletes. But now is the time to get into the exercise habit. Your body will get energy from whatever calories you put into it. But if you sit doing nothing, there is not much your bones, tendons, and muscles can do to keep themselves in shape. You've got to get up. You've got to move. It's good for your body and for *you*. And, interestingly, we now know that exercise stimulates the release of *endorphins*, which elevate our mood and sense of well-being. It's true, exercise is the ultimate natural high. So, grab your Rollerblades, go swimming, go ice-skating, play soccer, go for a run, a hike, or a long walk—just do *something*!

Two

The Zen of Acne

*L*et's face it—no pun intended—the hardest part about having pimples is that they appear on our faces. If pimples were confined to only our backs and chests or any other area that could be covered, they might not be such a big deal. But it is their prime location that makes them so tough to handle.

After all, our faces are what we present to the world. Here is all you need to know about taking care of your skin, and making peace with the face the world sees.

So, what is acne? Where does it come from? And how can we make it go away? *Acne* is the term for a condition in which numerous pimples appear on the face or other parts of the body, particularly the chest and the back. These pimples may be red lumps, whiteheads, or blackheads. But the pimples that show up on our faces don't begin there at all. *We* may look at a pimple as the beginning of a nightmare, but it is really the end result of a biological process that begins in our *sebaceous glands* (which produce oil) and is triggered by the hormones that surge through our system as we develop into women and men. This is the way it works:

1. During puberty, hormones stimulate the production of lots of oil.
2. The hair follicles get stopped up.
3. Bacteria get into the act, and there you have it—pimples!

What Causes Acne?

The major hormone that causes teenage acne is *androgen*—present in growing girls and growing boys. Boys produce much more androgen in the preteen and teenage years and, therefore, usually have worse cases of acne than most girls do, though this is not always true. Anyway, no one gets off the hook—boys and girls both suffer. It's one of the annoying but unavoidable parts of growing up.

What Can Make Acne Worse?

THE MENSTRUAL CYCLE Although there are a lot of myths about acne, it's true that the changes in your hormonal levels as

THE PIMPLE ITSELF

When the hair follicles in your skin become plugged and those plugs become irritated or infected, the result is acne. Hair grows all over your body, so there are hair follicles all over your skin, including on your face. Each and every hair follicle contains *sebaceous glands.* These glands produce an oil called sebum. The job of sebum is to lubricate both your hair and your skin.

Pimples form when sebum and dead skin cells are being produced faster than they can exit the hair follicle or pore. Think of it as one of Mother Nature's most unattractive traffic jams. A pileup occurs when the sebum and dead cells harden into a cheesy, white mass or plug. This plug causes the wall of the follicle to bulge, which creates a *whitehead.* When the pore remains open, this plug may darken, forming a *blackhead.* Blackheads are neither caused nor colored by dirt. They're just...blackheads. If the follicle wall ruptures, bacteria invade your skin. The resultant infection is called a pimple. Ruptures that are very deep within your skin will form boil-like infections. These are called *cysts* and can sometimes develop into a condition called *cystic acne.*

your period approaches can make your skin problems worse.

STRESS   When we go through rough times, our bodies react. If we're overly worried, overworked, or exhausted, our bodies feel it. It's harder to fight off colds and sickness when we are stressed-out. And most of us who have acne notice that our faces seem to break out more when we are going through difficult times.

HEREDITY   How prone you are to acne can be determined by your genes. Skin type—oily or dry—is inherited. If your mom or dad had acne, there's a good chance you will, too.

DIET   Although the jury is still out on whether foods play a role in causing acne or making it worse, we do know that diet plays an important role in health. It's important to eat a relatively healthful diet in order to be strong and healthy. But some of the old theories about junk food have been thrown out. Chocolate is no longer Public Enemy Number One when it comes to zits.

What about oily foods? Again, many doctors are no longer convinced that these foods cause acne. The final few words on the subject: It may be possible, but it's not probable. The truth is that you don't want to eat too much junk food for reasons of health, but a serving of french fries or a candy bar, here and there, is not going to affect your skin. So, if you eat french fries one evening and end up with a pimple the next morning, it's at least some consolation that the two events are unrelated. Still, if you find you *consistently* break out after eating a particular food, then omit it from your diet.

WEATHER   Hot and humid weather causes some people to break out, while a dry and sunny climate may improve the skin. However, this does not give you license to stay out in the sun all day to "burn out" your acne. Research points to the harmful long-term effects of sun on the skin. Being in the sun for long periods of time without wearing sun block can cause not only early aging but also cancer. And ultimately, tanning can make your acne worse. Your body responds to the drying effects of the sun and produces more oil to lubricate it. This gives more opportunity for plugged pores and . . . *pimples.*

What Can I Do to Clear Up Acne?

There's no one miracle treatment, but perhaps the one thing most doctors agree on is the benefits of drinking lots of water (at least eight glasses a day). Although drinking lots of water can't prevent acne, it helps keep your system healthy and keeps you from getting dehydrated—all of which is good for your skin.

YOUR PERSONAL SKIN CARE ROUTINE

Taking good care of your skin can help prevent your acne from getting worse. It will also help you feel you've got some power over a situation that sometimes seems out of control. Taking care of yourself will help you feel good about yourself.

You should wash your face at least twice a day, morning and night. If you play team sports or exercise frequently, you should wash your face after every workout to avoid giving sweat and bacteria any chance to further clog your pores.

There are many cleansing products to choose from— from ordinary soap to specialty skin cleansers, astringents, and facial masks, among others. Rather than becoming over-whelmed by the choices, you may want to make a project of researching which products are best for your particular skin type and what routine is best for you.

Oily Skin

Wash your face two or three times a day but no more. Too much washing can strip away the natural oils from your skin. This may irritate the skin, causing the sebaceous glands to produce even more oil. You may also want to experiment with using a drying mask once a week to see if this helps to reduce excessive oil in your skin.

If you have blackheads, whiteheads, pimples, or all of these, you'll also want to try using a product that contains *benzoyl peroxide,* which is considered the most effective over-the-counter acne medication. Benzoyl peroxide does two very important things: It dries out acne *and* it kills bacteria. The gel form is most effective, and it comes in different strengths: 2 percent, 5 percent, and 10 percent solutions. You'll want to start with a weaker strength and work up to a stronger strength if needed. Talk to your pediatrician about this. She or he can help start you on a sensible routine.

Your Skin Type
A SIMPLE TEST

The only things you need to find out what skin type you have once and for all are a little bit of time, some blotting paper, and a mild soap. Just follow these steps:

- Take your blotting paper and cut it into four pieces. Label the pieces NOSE, CHEEKS, CHIN, and FOREHEAD.
- Wash your face with a mild soap and lukewarm water. Do not apply any astringent or moisturizer after you dry your face.
- Wait a couple of hours—read a book, listen to music, call a girlfriend, help your father with dinner.
- Now hold each paper against the designated area and count to ten . . . slowly.
- Look at the papers in bright light. Any papers that are totally dry tell you that your skin is *dry* in those areas. Any papers with a faint residue of oil that's hardly visible indicate your skin is *normal* in those areas. If you can clearly see an oily residue on the papers, your skin is *oily* in those areas, and a heavy residue indicates you have *very oily* skin.

If you have truly dry skin, all the papers will be dry. For combination skin, the cheeks are usually dry and one to three of the other papers will come away with an oily residue. For very oily skin, even the cheeks may show an oily residue.

Dry Skin

If regular soap dries your skin out, try using a soap especially formulated for dry skin, or a facial cleanser. A soothing toner after washing, followed by an oil-free moisturizer, will also help keep your skin from getting dry and flaky.

Combination Skin

Many people have combination skin, which is oily in some areas (generally the nose and/or chin) and dry in others (generally the cheeks). After washing with a gentle soap or oil-free cleanser, apply an oil-free moisturizer to dry areas but skip the oily areas. Many companies now make products for combination, or "confused," skin that both absorb oil and provide an oil-free moisturizer at the same time. Such a product can make your job easier.

Some of the many product lines that offer a variety of skin care options include: Neutrogena, Oil of Olay, Almay, Aveda, Clinique, Aveeno, Noxema, and Origins. As with any new purchase, read the labels and check out the ingredients. Many of the inexpensive brands are *just as good* as the expensive ones.

What's *My* **Hair** *Got to Do with It?*

In your skin care strategy, you'll want to remember that, unless you've got a buzz cut, your hair is the thing that's most "in your face," especially if you have bangs or you wear your hair long around your face. If your hair is oily and you let it get dirty, all of that oil and dirt rubs off on your face, helping

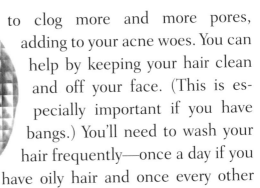

to clog more and more pores, adding to your acne woes. You can help by keeping your hair clean and off your face. (This is especially important if you have bangs.) You'll need to wash your hair frequently—once a day if you have oily hair and once every other day if your hair is dry. If you use a styling gel, mousse, or hair spray, try to rinse it out of your hair every night before you go to bed.

To Squeeze or Not to Squeeze?

The answer is: *Not.* The answer is: *No way.* The answer is: *Never.* So, how come everybody does it? The question is: *Who can resist?* Presidents, rock stars, movie stars, scientists, kings, queens, astronauts, and ballplayers—all have probably squeezed a pimple at least once in their lives. So, while we'll tell you not to, we'll also tell you the least damaging way to do it if you feel you must.

First, the *reason* you shouldn't squeeze your pimples is because squeezing only makes them *redder, bigger,* and *more unsightly.* Squeezing can also cause *scarring.* And a scar will last a lifetime, whereas a pimple at least will eventually go away. Squeezing pimples can also be very painful. And once you start to squeeze, it's hard to stop—and there's got to be more to life than staring at yourself in the mirror and squeezing zits. At least we hope there is!

But if you must squeeze, here are some don'ts and dos that will help you minimize the damage.

Don'ts!

DON'T pop your pimples right before school, or a date, or a dance, or a party, or the school play, or your first speech as a candidate for class president. You'll end up with very obvious, swollen red spots that can't be camouflaged.

DON'T *ever* touch your pimples with a sharp instrument, such as tweezers or a needle. You can do permanent damage.

DON'T stay home just because you have a pimple!

Dos!

DO wash your hands and face before you touch your face.

DO open your pores by putting a warm, wet washcloth over your face at least five or six times in a row. But don't let it get too hot—you don't want to burn yourself.

DO use cotton balls or squares when you squeeze, and press very gently.

DO wrap some ice in a dishcloth and press it on the affected areas afterward to reduce the swelling.

DO use benzoyl peroxide or salicylic solution (present in most acne creams and gels) on the affected areas afterward.

DO leave your face alone, giving it time to heal. Talk to a friend on the phone, listen to music, read a book, or finish your homework.

SOME WILD AND CRAZY FACTS ABOUT ACNE

★ *The glands of our lives:* There are thousands and thousands of oil glands on the face. That's a lot of oil.

★ *Acne remedies have been around since ancient times:* Barley flour, bean paste, various herbs, and oils were used to treat pimples.

★ *Pus—you may hate living with it, but you can't live without it:* Pus is what your body produces while it is fighting certain kinds of infections. It's composed of tissue fluid, which contains bacteria and *leukocytes,* the white corpuscles of the blood. Pus is usually yellowish. As unattractive as pus is, it may help to think that it results from your body's efforts to heal itself. If acne is how your body battles infection, think of pus as a necessary casualty in a battle well fought.

CONSULTING A DERMATOLOGIST WHEN MORE HELP IS NEEDED

If the over-the-counter medications aren't helping to clear up your skin or if your acne is so severe that it is spoiling the quality of your life, then it's time to see a dermatologist. *Dermatologists* are doctors whose specialty is the skin. Your pediatrician can recommend someone for you to see. If your parents tell you that your acne is "only a phase" and "it will pass," this is one time to disagree. It will certainly pass more quickly and you'll have less scarring and be less affected by it emotionally if you get some help from a doctor who treats acne.

If you suggest seeing a dermatologist and your parents explain to you that such treatment is very expensive, you might want to ask them to look into your family medical coverage. These days many insurance companies are being very careful about what medical expenses are covered. However, if your family participates in a managed care plan, generally all you need to do is have your pediatrician or family physician recommend that you see a dermatologist, and at least a portion of the specialist's fee will be covered by insurance.

How a Dermatologist Can Help

Help *is* on the way when you take that step to see a dermatologist. The dermatologist will examine your skin and discuss a course of treatment with you. She will recommend a skin care routine and what products, cleansers, and medicine you should use for your skin. With your permission, she may drain your pimples. If your acne is serious, she may also prescribe an antibiotic, such as tetracycline, to fight the infection (your pimples) from the inside. Remember, the earlier you get help for acne, the better you will feel both inside and out.

There are a variety of topical treatments (applied directly to the skin) that your dermatologist might recommend.

BENZOYL PEROXIDE As we said before, *benzoyl peroxide* is considered one of the safest and most effective of readily available treatments for acne. It's very successful at

49

attacking the bacteria that's deep down inside the hair follicles. Even better, in many cases benzoyl peroxide is the only
treatment necessary.

SALICYLIC ACID   *Salicylic acid* may be used alone or
in combination with a sulfur product. No one is quite sure exactly how salicylic acid helps the skin, but most experts agree
that it works as an anti-inflammatory agent. Salicylic acid
should only be used in concentrations of 0.5 to 2.0 percent.

RETIN-A   *Retin-A* is a vitamin A derivative that is very
effective in treating acne, but it must be prescribed by a dermatologist. Unless your acne is very serious, most dermatologists will not prescribe Retin-A because of the possible side
effects. If you are using Retin-A, your skin is more apt to become very dry and sensitive. You'll have to wear sunscreen—
number thirty at least—whenever you're outdoors. You'll also
have to avoid any astringents, toners, or abrasive cleansers.
Forgetting any of these precautions will probably make your
skin worse, not better. Also, never share your prescription
with someone else, and never use somebody else's Retin-A.
You and your skin may be sorry if you do.

Remember, none of these treatments works overnight, and
it's important to be patient and not give up. To see results, you
have to be diligent about continuing your routine.

Concealing Your Zits

Okay, so now you have a healthy skin care routine. Like everything else in life, it will be subject to change. As your skin

changes, you can continue to experiment with what works and what doesn't. But how does makeup fit into your regimen? Very well, and here's why: Makeup formulas get better and better every year. Applied correctly, makeup should barely be noticeable. Heavy pancake makeup only draws attention to both the makeup and the skin problems beneath it. The point we want to emphasize is that when we talk about makeup here, we are not talking about *makeovers*. Instead, we are talking about using some of the excellent products on the market that can *cover* and *conceal* zits. When used properly, makeup can work wonders by hiding red areas and bumps. Makeup can help you to feel less self-conscious and therefore more secure.

Where to Start

There are many kinds of makeup, and each can serve a different function. There are makeup sticks to cover zits and scars. There are liquid foundations and powdered foundations, sheer foundations and thick foundations. Ask for advice in the drugstore or ask your friends what they use.

Makeup does *not* have to be expensive to be of good quality. You will need to be a thoughtful consumer and read labels. Often the same ingredients are used in different products, yet one brand is expensive while another is reasonable. Do make sure that you are using oil-free makeup, because it will not clog your pores. Powder, if it's oil free, will not clog your pores, either, and is fine to use as well. Try to choose a makeup that is *noncomedogenic,* meaning that it's formulated not to clog your pores. It's a good idea when trying out a product to keep a list of the ingredients if they are not on the tube or the bottle itself. This is so that if you have a bad reaction to the makeup, you can begin to figure out which ingredient is the culprit.

How to Use Makeup

Finding the right color is key. A saleswoman in a drugstore or a department store can be extremely knowledgeable and helpful, both in choosing the right color for you and in teaching you the best way to apply makeup. Usually all you need is a dab of makeup on the zit itself or a touch of powder to take away the oily shine on your nose. It's amazing how a touch of the right makeup to cover up a zit can really help you feel more confident about presenting your face to the world.

The Acne Blues

What if you are just starting out your new skin care routine, or haven't begun it yet, and the pimples on your face make you want to hide? Well, hang in there because you are not alone. Remember, most people have had zits at one time or another. And it's also important to remember always that although we might look at our faces as if they were under a microscope, nobody else does. Our friends are glad to see us because they love who we are, and pimples can't change that. But one thing that might be difficult is parents who try so desperately to spare their children the pain of acne that they make the situation worse by going overboard. You know: "Don't pick." "Did you wash your face?" "No, you can't have french fries." "*You* should not be eating chocolate." Because acne is hereditary, parents often have suffered from acne themselves and so try very hard to make the experience different for their children. In the process of trying too hard, however, they may alienate you by scrutinizing you all the time and making you feel far more self-conscious than you already do.

If this is what's happening between you and your parents, talk to them. Explain how and when they make you feel bad. Tell them you know they mean well, but sometimes they overdo it. Most parents will appreciate what their kids have to say. And by helping your parents see the situation, you're helping yourself.

Battling the Blues

When we feel there is something wrong with our face—and a single pimple can make us feel this—we feel *vulnerable*. It's as if a spotlight is shining directly on that big unsightly pimple and the rest of who we are vanishes. But the truth is that we are not our pimples. They are just an extremely annoying and often painful part of growing up.

So, how do we deal with these negative feelings that are caused by having acne?

BE A DETECTIVE, NOT A CRITIC
Remember, *knowledge is power*—so get to know yourself. Be on the lookout for clues to what makes your acne better or worse. Keep a clue notebook, if you want to. Write everything down and then see if you can solve the mystery of what makes your acne worse and what works to make it better. At least you'll feel like you're doing something to help. If you learn that your skin breaks out

- before or during your period
- during exam week
- before a music recital
- when you are under any kind of stress

then you know these are your *vulnerable times.*

Try to be especially kind to yourself during these trying days. This is *not* the time to give in to negative feelings.

WHAT ACNE CAN AND CAN'T DO
Acne *can* make you cry if you let it get to you. Acne can make you want to hide your face. Acne can make you want to disappear. Acne can make you angry. Acne can make you think things are worse than they really are.

Acne *can't* stop you from getting the part in the school play, getting into the college of your choice, dancing, singing, painting, playing baseball and basketball, acing a history test, solving an algebra problem. It also can't prevent you from blading, running, studying ballet, ice-skating, going to the

Don'ts !

DON'T sit up on the edge of the bathroom sink and pick away at your zits.

DON'T give yourself a radical haircut or hairstyle.

DON'T pick a fight with your best friend.

DON'T make a mental list of all your shortcomings.

DON'T compare yourself unfavorably to anyone else.

zit

zit

Dos !

DO take a long hot bath or shower.

DO try that new rosemary shampoo sample.

DO wear comfortable clothes.

DO buy that CD you've been saving up for.

DO borrow that exciting mystery from the library.

DO spend time with people you love.

DO go for a walk, play basketball, dance around your room. (Exercise is a natural antidepressant.)

DO read a story to a younger child.

DO get involved in your community.

DO shift your focus away from the surface of your skin to the world around you.

movies, being a good friend and having good friends, falling in love or having someone fall in love with you.

THE ZEN OF ACNE

We asked girls what they think of when they hear the word *zen*, and their answers include: "Buddhism," "little zen gardens," "harmony," "peace," and "tranquillity."

Zen Buddhism was founded in India more than two thousand years ago by Prince Shakyamuni Buddha, who sought a spiritual life. In his book *Taking the Path of Zen*, Robert Aitken says: "Yamada Roshi has said: The practice of Zen is forgetting the self in the act of uniting with something." Instead of concentrating on your zits when you look in the mirror, concentrate and unite with your eyes; they're more important. They allow you to see everything. Go look at a mountain or a bird, your best friend or your boyfriend, your parents or your baby brother, your favorite book or movie. You've got more control than you think, if you'll just shift your focus. You can do it.

On really bad "zit days," it may help to have a mantra to get you through. (A mantra is a sound, a word, or a phrase that you say over and over again to calm yourself, which may help you to concentrate and meditate.) Here are some starters:

- *This too shall pass.*
- *Beauty's only skin deep.*
- *Life goes on.*

What's Going On on the Inside

As we grow up, there are going to be days when we like the idea of being human and others when we don't like it one bit. It's normal every now and then to say to yourself, "Gross, is that me?" But understanding how and why the human body functions as it does can help you through those "cringe moments" and may even help you say to yourself, "Wow! I get it. My body is amazing."

Your Amazing Body

No matter how many diagrams of our internal organs we may see, the 206 bones that make up the human skeleton, the folds and coils of gray matter that compose our brain—our bodies are pretty astounding, even impossible to believe.

What's in there anyway?

❋ Well, there's your *heart,* which sends the blood you need to every finger and toe. Your heart is a pump—and what a pump. Your heart pumps *five or more quarts of blood per minute!* And in a single day your heart will pump about *two thousand gallons of blood* through the arteries, veins, and capillaries of your circulatory system. Now, that's quite a pump!

❋ There's your *brain,* which is composed of approximately *a hundred billion neurons* (nerve cells). Your brain receives input from all your body parts and the outside world, and it is your means of transmitting messages to your body as well as to your friends. Your brain makes you think and stimulates your imagination, but it also sends impulses to every part of your body—telling the arms to move, the mouth to smile, the legs to run, among other things. And this most complex organ weighs…guess how much? *About three pounds*—quite an amazing "machine"!

❋ There's also your *lungs.* With the help of your brain, your lungs make it possible for you to breathe. Your breath then carries oxygen to your heart and blood, allowing your heart to pump oxygen through the blood to all the organs of your body, including your brain—the central switchboard—

which needs the blood to get the oxygen it requires to function and make the whole system work.

※ And there are your *intestines,* which digest the food you eat and eliminate the waste the body makes, to keep the body healthy. There are also many other internal organs that help orchestrate the bodily functions.

What's all this got to do with growing up; getting your period; getting breasts, hips, and zits; falling in love; falling in hate; feeling cranky; feeling jittery; fighting with your best friend; staying up late; and never, never, never getting enough sleep? Plenty.

Located at the base of the brain is a gland that's essential when it comes to puberty, the *pituitary gland.* The pituitary gland is an important part of the *endocrine system.* Composed of glands, the endocrine system serves as the signaling network for most of the body's functions. It does this by regulating the hormone levels in the body. The pituitary gland is responsible for many of these hormones, including the sex hormones that let your body know it's time to start growing up.

60

YOUR REPRODUCTIVE ORGANS

From when you are about eight or even younger, your body starts getting ready for the time you will be able to reproduce, or have a baby. (This does not mean there's a rule that says you *must* have a baby one day; it only means that your body is getting ready should you decide to do so.) This *getting ready* part is where hormones come in. They prepare your girl's body to begin the process of becoming a woman's body.

Picture the inside of your body just prior to puberty as a darkened room. Then one by one your hormones begin to turn on the lights. Each of us is different, so no one can tell you exactly when this will happen. But, rest assured, it *will* happen when it is supposed to. There are many, many different hormones in the body, but the ones that determine when a girl begins puberty are *estrogen* and *progesterone*.

THE OVARIES
You have two *ovaries,* one to the right and one to the left of your uterus. Inside the ovaries are the *ova,* which means "eggs." (One egg is called an *ovum.*) All baby girls are born with over a million ova, more eggs than they'll ever need for life—very practical. By the time a girl starts to menstruate, she has about four hundred thousand eggs remaining—still far more than she'll ever need.

During puberty one of the jobs of the hormone estrogen is to help the eggs mature. When an egg is mature it is released. Some months one ovary releases one egg. Other months the other ovary releases an egg. This is called *ovulation*. Ovulation allows your body the opportunity to become pregnant.

THE FALLOPIAN TUBES
The four-inch *fallopian tubes* are like the roads or tunnels of the female reproductive system. The eggs travel through the fallopian tubes on their way to the uterus. At the end of the fallopian tubes are the *fimbria*, which is Latin for "fingers." The fimbria look a bit like the tentacles of an underwater plant.

When an egg is released from the ovary, the fimbria's job is to sweep the egg into the fallopian tube. Inside the fallopian tube, tiny hairs called *cilia* wave back and forth like sea grass, moving the egg along. It takes about four days for the egg to reach the uterus. If the egg has been fertilized, it will implant itself in the walls of the uterus.

THE UTERUS
The *uterus*, also known as the womb, lies between the ovaries and fallopian tubes and above the vagina.

The uterus is our first home. We each find our way there as tiny fertilized eggs. Think of the softest, most comfortable bed in the world—that's what the lining of the uterus must feel like to the egg, which is going to lodge there. The thick, soft, blood-filled lining of the uterus has all the nutrients we need to grow. And for the next nine months or so, until the day we are born, the uterus is our house.

In addition to being a perfect home for the developing fetus, another amazing characteristic of the uterus is its great capacity to expand. During pregnancy the uterus stretches to accommodate the growing life.

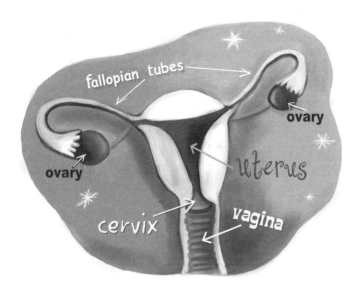

fallopian tubes

ovary

ovary

uterus

cervix

vagina

THE CERVIX
The *cervix* is the neck at the bottom portion of the uterus. It has a hole in it called the *cervical os* that connects the uterus to the vagina, and it is a very important opening. When a woman is pregnant, the cervix acts like a bottle cap, remaining closed until it is time for her baby to be born. Then, when a woman is in labor, the cervix opens, stretching wider to about ten centimeters to allow the baby to pass through.

THE VAGINA
The *vagina* is the canal that leads from the inside of a girl's or a woman's body to the outside. It is also called the birth canal because it is where a baby passes through to be born.

The vagina has very muscular walls that can expand or contract. During puberty it's normal to see a clear or milky fluid that drips out of the vagina. This is called a *vaginal discharge*. The reason for the discharge is that the vagina not only sheds some of its cells but must also wash these cells away. This keeps the vagina clean and healthy. By the way, it's normal to have beige or yellowish stains on your underwear from these discharges.

YEAST INFECTIONS

Some discharges indicate that you might have an infection, such as a *yeast infection*. Yeast is a type of fungus that lives in our body. Certain conditions can cause us to produce more yeast than we need. Yeast infections in the vagina are quite common among growing girls and women. The medical term for yeast infection is *Candida vulvovaginitis.*

Yeast grows most readily in a warm, moist environment. Sitting around in a wet bathing suit, for example, can encourage the beginning of a yeast infection. Wearing nylon, which is a synthetic material that doesn't "breathe," can also cause or exacerbate a yeast infection. Choose underwear that has a cotton crotch.

Taking antibiotics can cause yeast infections. This is because antibiotics kill off the healthy bacteria in your vagina and allow any yeast present to overgrow. So when you're taking an antibiotic, try to eat yogurt with live cultures every day. This helps to maintain healthy bacteria working in your system to keep the yeast fungus from reproducing.

If you have a yeast infection, you'll usually notice a thick, white odorless discharge that may look a bit like cottage cheese. The inside of your vagina will feel itchy, and the lips of your vagina may be a little red and sore and may be itchy as well.

A yeast infection will not go away by itself; it will only get worse and probably make you more uncomfortable. Proper medication will clear it up quickly. In fact, the antifungal medications you need are available without prescription. But vaginal itching can also be caused by something more serious than a fungal infection. So don't go out and buy over-the-counter medication until you've seen a doctor, just in case your symptoms signal something other than a yeast infection. If you notice a discharge that you've never seen before, especially one that smells unpleasant and is causing itching inside your vagina, you should tell your mother, father, or another adult with whom you are close, and have a checkup by your doctor.

WHEN MENSTRUATION BEGINS

When a girl has her period, or *menstruates,* menstrual blood drips out of her vagina. Where does this blood come from? Well, you remember that when a girl *ovulates* (releases an egg), her uterus has been busy building up a thick lining of blood and tissue, which would become home to an egg if it were fertilized by a sperm. Most of the time the egg isn't fertilized, so this rich nutrient-filled lining is not needed. So, the lining begins to break down and drip out of the vagina. The flow of blood and tissue is called *menstruation,* or having your period. Menstruation is a cleansing process for your uterus.

Many girls wonder if you can see the egg come out when you menstruate. The answer is no. Not only is the egg too tiny—the size of a grain of sand—but when an egg is not fertilized, it dies within twenty-four hours. It will have dissolved by the time the period begins.

When
Will I Get
My Period?

If only there were some way of knowing *exactly* when you were going to get your period....If someone could say, "Okay, Jane, on June twelfth next year at exactly ten minutes and thirty-nine seconds after eight A.M., you will get your period," that would take away a lot of worry. But, of course, nature doesn't work that way. It *does* give us pretty good clues, though. And just as spring cannot come right before winter, certain changes in the body have to take place before you get your period.

What Comes Before

There are clues that signal that you'll get your period sometime within a year or two:

✳ **Pubic hair** usually begins to appear about a year or two before your period arrives.
✳ **Breast development** usually has occurred, which means your breasts are past the budding stage and are almost fully developed.
✳ **Vaginal discharges** usually begin two years to six months before your first period.

During the *months* before your first period, you may notice an increase in white or yellowish vaginal fluid. This is due to your changing hormones and is a natural part of development.

In the *weeks* before your first period, you may notice that your breasts feel tender or even sore, and you may feel cramping in your abdomen. These are called *premenstrual cramps*. As the uterus works to push out its lining of blood and tissue, you may feel cramps. The first time you get cramps, you might think you have a stomachache, but you'll soon be able to tell the difference. (The uterus is *below* the stomach, and cramps cause an achy, tugging sensation there.) Some girls have more severe cramps than others. Some girls hardly notice them at all. And every month is different. So if you have bad cramps the first time, it doesn't mean you will the next time.

Sometimes girls have a little diarrhea the day before their period or during the first day of their period (or both). And some girls may feel nauseous or get headaches. This is normal, too.

PMS

PMS stands for *premenstrual syndrome*. The shift in a girl's and a woman's hormones a few days before her period can cause her to feel cranky, irritable, weepy, depressed, supersensitive, bloated, or ravenously hungry, among other things. And PMS can cause painful cramping. Of course, not everyone has mood changes or food cravings or cramps at this time of the month, but many girls and women do.

Luckily, there are a number of things that may help. Exercise, relaxing baths or showers, using a hot-water bottle or a heating pad, cutting down on salty foods and chocolate, taking four hundred units of vitamin E, and getting extra sleep really help. Calcium, which is extremely important for our bones, can also help reduce PMS symptoms. Twelve hundred milligrams a day is recommended by the *New England Journal of Medicine*.

If you have extreme pain or bloating, or both, discuss the situation with friends, your mother or father, or other adults you trust. You might consider taking an over-the-counter pain medication, or make an appointment with your doctor to discuss the situation further. It's very important that you get help and not suffer.

The First Time

No matter how well prepared you are for getting your period, almost everyone is still surprised when it happens. And whenever we have high expectations, there is always the potential for a certain amount—or some might say a lot!—of disappointment.

Menarche is the word for your first period, the beginning of your menstrual cycle, which will be part of the rhythm of your life until about the age of fifty. You may have your first period at any time between the ages of eight and seventeen, and whatever age you are, that's what is normal for you.

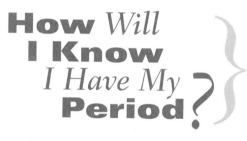

How Will I Know I Have My Period?

Even if we know what a period is, the first time we get it, most of us ask ourselves, "Is this the real thing?" We may notice a bit of brownish stuff in our underpants or we may find a trace of pinkish blood on the toilet paper when we're wiping ourselves. *Is this it?* we wonder.

What can make it all the more confusing is that sometimes this first sighting of blood (be it brown, red, or pinkish red) is pretty much all that comes with our first period. And then a month later, or maybe two, we notice spots of blood again. This time the blood will continue to appear over a few days.

Of course, some girls recognize their period for what it is, right away. Their blood may be obviously red and they may find that they are bleeding quite heavily for a few days in a row. But whatever the amount of blood there is and whatever its color and however long the bleeding lasts, a girl can rest assured that the first sign of blood means that she has begun to menstruate.

How Much Blood Will There Be?

Your period can last anywhere from two to seven days. During this time, you may lose only one-quarter to one-half cup of blood and tissue. But it might seem like a lot more than that at first.

What Does It Feel Like to Menstruate?

When you have your period, the blood comes out in drips, some big (these might feel like a gush) and some small. It's not a nonstop flow of blood. And you can't start or stop the flow of blood the way you can control the flow of urine when you're peeing. Because each period is made up of blood and tissue, it's normal to see small clumps of blood.

Light, Medium, and Heavy Flow

The first few days of a girl's period usually have the heaviest flow, which means there is more blood. But as the days pass, the flow gets lighter and lighter, until one day there's no more bleeding. As your period ends, it's normal to see small clumps of darker blood. This is tissue from your uterine lining.

Some girls have light periods, some have medium, and

The Stages of Your Cycle

Just as there are phases of the moon, there are phases of the menstrual cycle, too—three to be exact. The first phase is one of *preparation,* when the lining of the uterus grows in case the egg, released at ovulation, is to be fertilized. The second phase, called the *secretary phase,* refers to the time of ovulation, when the female body stays ready to feed a fertilized egg. The third phase is *menstruation,* when your body sheds the uterine lining it no longer needs because the egg released was not fertilized. And then the cycle begins again.

some have heavy ones. Some girls start out with a heavy flow for a day or two, skip a medium flow, and go right to a light flow. Everyone is different. And what happens to you is normal for your body. Your flow also might change in terms of lightness or heaviness from month to month. This happens to lots of girls and women.

What to Use: Pads, Tampons, and Panty Liners

When you begin to menstruate, you can choose between a sanitary pad and a tampon to absorb the blood. Actually, it doesn't have to be an either-or decision. Many of us use both. We may use tampons during the day and then switch to pads at night. And some women use tampons and pads at the same time if they're having a very heavy flow. Whatever you prefer

to use is the right choice, and both pads and tampons have their advantages.

APPLYING A PAD
Pads are a cinch to use. Many have adhesive tape, which helps them stick to your underwear. All you do is pull off the strip of paper covering the tape and then place the pad tape-side (the sticky side) down on the inside crotch of your underpants. Some pads have adhesive wings that wrap around the crotch of your underpants. These help keep the pad from moving out of place. Pads come in a variety of shapes, lengths, and degrees of thickness. *Maxi* are the thickest ones, and *mini* are the thinnest. You'll probably want to try out different brands and sizes to see which is the most comfortable.

When your flow is heavier, you will need to change your pad more frequently. As you adjust to your period, you will be able to tell the difference between your light and heavy days.

But it's a good idea to change your pad every three to four hours, to avoid accidents, for health reasons, for sanitary reasons, and just so you feel plain old clean and comfortable. When you change your pad, wrap the used one in toilet paper and throw it in the garbage. Do not flush it because the pad could clog the toilet.

It might help to know that every one of us has had experiences with leaking in our underpants, on bedsheets, and even through our clothes. And sure, it can be embarrassing. But it's just part of having your period. *Cold water*, not hot, works best to get out bloodstains. Soak the soiled item in cold water, or hold it under a stream of cold water until the blood runs out.

Whether you choose a tampon or a pad when the blood is flowing, a panty liner or panty shield is another option for the very light days at the end of your period. These are much thinner and lighter than sanitary pads.

What Clothes to Wear

Most of us have more trouble choosing what to wear when we have or are getting our period. These basic tips might help you choose:

❋ Pick something comfortable.

❋ Don't think you're being silly if you change your clothes twice or more.

❋ Wear jeans, dark pants, or a dark skirt if you're worried about the blood leaking through your underwear.

❋ Keep a dark sweatshirt at school to wrap around your waist in case you leak through.

You hardly know you're wearing one, but you do know you're protected until the blood has completely stopped flowing.

By the way, it's a good idea to have a few pads or tampons in your backpack or bag so you're prepared, just in case, when you think your period is coming. But don't worry if you don't have a pad or a tampon when you start, because you can do what thousands of girls have done before you and will continue to do in a pinch: Wad up toilet paper and stick it in your underpants.

If you get your period at school, you can get a pad or a tampon from the vending machines in the girls' bathroom, or even from a teacher or the school office or nurse.

USING A TAMPON

The advantage to using tampons is that they allow you to swim and to participate in other rigorous sports, even on the heaviest days of your period. Some girls who have just begun to menstruate find it difficult to insert a tampon, but others adjust immediately. It's a good idea to use

nondeodorant tampons, because the perfume in a deodorant might irritate your vagina.

Here's a thought that might give you comfort: This is one life skill you get to learn in total privacy. You don't have to worry. Nobody's watching. You can make mistakes. You can use as many tampons as you need to get it right.

The trick to inserting a tampon is to *breathe deeply and relax.* When you are tense, the muscles in your body get tight. The tenser you are, the harder it will be to put in a tampon. Here are some tips:

※ Wash your hands.

※ Breathe in deeply, then exhale slowly to relax.

※ Use the slimmest tampon, at least for your first few times.

※ Look at the instruction diagram that comes in the box of tampons. It will show you how to insert one.

※ Try putting a dab of a lubricant, such as K-Y jelly, on the tip of the tampon. (*This can make all the difference in the world because it helps the tampon slide easily into the vagina.*)

※ Hold a mirror up to your vagina so you can see where the tampon goes in.

Some girls find it easier to put one foot up on the toilet when they put in a tampon, and some girls prefer to be sitting on the toilet. Unwrap the tampon and gently slide the applicator into the vagina, angling it up and toward your back. Take your time. Once you feel the tampon is in place, pull the applicator out. You may not get it right the first few times. That's okay. We've all been there. And we all got the hang of it … eventually.

CHOOSING A TAMPON

Once you've decided to use a tampon, then you have to choose which type to use.

There are three types of tampons: One comes with a cardboard applicator, one with a plastic applicator, and one with no applicator at all—you use your fingers to guide the tampon. This is the hardest kind of tampon to insert, and it's a good idea for beginners to skip it until they learn the ropes. The cardboard or plastic applicators are easier to use, because the cardboard or plastic helps the tampon to slip into the vagina more easily. And the tampon of choice for most girls is the one with a plastic applicator that has a rounded tip.

THROWING AWAY YOUR USED TAMPON

Okay, you've gotten that first tampon in; you've pulled the string and taken it out—and even inserted a fresh one, with no problem. NOW WHAT DO YOU DO WITH THE USED ONE? The best way to dispose of a tampon is to wrap it in toilet paper and throw it in the garbage can (same goes for the applicator, by the way). Some tampons are advertised as "flushable." But even flushable tampons can cause plumbing problems. You can save yourself, and the toilet, some stress by using the garbage instead.

Toxic Shock Syndrome

Toxic shock syndrome, or TSS, is so rare that we considered not discussing it. It's scary, too. But toxic shock syndrome is almost 100 percent preventable, and that's why we're telling you about it here—so you can take the necessary steps to avoid TSS.

Toxic shock is caused by a bacterium. (Ninety percent of cases occur in women who use tampons. One cause can be not changing tampons often enough.) The symptoms include high fever, very watery diarrhea, and vomiting. A sore throat and aching muscles may also be associated with toxic shock. Because the syndrome is sometimes associated with the improper use of tampons, obviously these symptoms occur while a girl is having her period.

Here's how to avoid toxic shock syndrome if you use tampons:

- Wash your hands each time you insert a tampon.
- Do not use superabsorbent tampons.
- Do not use tampons the entire time you're having your period. Use pads when you can, and particularly toward the end of your period, when the flow of blood has almost stopped.
- Change your tampon often. This way you avoid forgetting you have a tampon in, which we've all done occasionally!
- Use a slender tampon or a regular tampon on heavy-flow days.
- Never leave a tampon in place for more than six hours.

Common Questions from Girls about
Using Tampons

Do I have to be a certain age to use a tampon?
No, it's safe to use a tampon whenever it is that you begin to menstruate.

How does a tampon stay in?
The walls of the vagina keep it in place.

Can the string break?
We've never heard of this happening. But if it does, you can gently insert your fingers into your vagina to pull the tampon out.

What if I can't find the string?
Sometimes the string of the tampon gets folded up inside the vagina. This is not a problem. You can use a finger to gently pull the string back down.

Can the tampon get lost?
No way. The vagina is only about four inches long from the vaginal opening.

And the tampon cannot escape through the tiny cervix and get lost in the uterus. The cervix protects the uterus from anything unwanted entering it. You can always crouch down and gently put your fingers inside your vagina to pull the tampon out.

Does it hurt to put in a tampon?
Sometimes, but just a little—*and only if you are not putting it in the right way.* It's all about putting the tampon in at the right angle. Don't push it up, but angle it up and back, toward your lower back.

Does it hurt to wear a tampon?
If the tampon is in properly, it won't hurt at all—in fact, you won't even feel it.

Am I able to pee when wearing a tampon?
Yes, because the tampon is inside your vagina and not inside your urethra, which carries the pee out of your body.

How do you know if a tampon is in the right way?
When a tampon fits and is inserted properly, you can't feel it. If you can feel it, that usually means it is not positioned high enough inside the vagina. If this is the case (and it sometimes happens even to women who have been using tampons for years), you just gently pull it out and insert a new tampon. Another reason a tampon might not feel comfortable is because it's too big. Tampons, like pads, come in different sizes and degrees of thickness: junior, slender, regular, and super.

Can you lose your virginity by using a tampon?
No. We repeat: No! A *virgin* is someone who has never had sexual intercourse.

WHO INVENTED THE *Tampon?*

Ancient women around the world were very resourceful. They created tamponlike absorbers out of softened papyrus, grass, vegetable fiber, and wool. The tampon as we know it was invented by Dr. Earle Haas in the 1930s. To protect the hygiene of girls and women as much as possible, he came up with the two-part applicator and the brilliant addition of the string to the tampon. The rest is history!

YOUR OWN CYCLE

Don't let the term *menarche,* or your first period, fool you into thinking that from now on, at the same time on the same day every month, you'll get your period.

During your first two years or so of menstruating, your periods may be quite irregular. You may get your period early one month, and you may skip your period altogether another month. Consider this first year or so to be a time of adjustment. It is a good idea to keep track, in a diary or a calendar, of when your period comes, so that you can determine the pattern of your cycle. Knowing when to expect your period makes it easier to cope with than being surprised by it.

Don't Be Alarmed
(Other Common Occurrences)

As we've said, the body doesn't always work as smoothly as your favorite CD. Or let's put it this way: Just as a CD may bump if it's dusty, so your body may skip a beat here and there. Don't be alarmed—there are many changes, internal and external, that are occurring in your body, and you're bound to end up facing some unexpected issues. Asking a grown-up you trust to help you cope with the surprises will make things easier. Puberty is a little like going to a new school. You're going to have to ask for directions at least once in a while, and the sooner you ask, the sooner you're going to know your way around.

Here are some very normal problems that girls may face.

MIGRAINE HEADACHES Some girls who have started getting their periods begin to get *migraine headaches* at that particular time of month. The only good news is that if you do get horrible headaches, you'll know that's a sign your period is coming and so you'll pack your bag or backpack with pads or tampons.

These very painful headaches usually pass after your first year or two of menstruation. Talk to your doctor, your school nurse, your mother or father, or some other knowledgeable grown-up about how to treat this problem. There are medications that can help relieve the symptoms if the headaches are very bad.

BLADDER INFECTIONS (UTIs) *Bladder* or *urinary tract infections* are not uncommon during the first year or two of menstruation. If you have a bladder infection, you need to see your doctor. The symptoms include frequent and painful urination, and sometimes cramping and pain in the lower abdomen. Drinking cranberry juice may help to treat the infections or prevent them, as may eating yogurt with live cultures. Drinking plenty of water is essential. But because a bladder infection won't go away by itself, you must see a doctor to treat it.

DYSMENORRHEA
Dysmenorrhea is the serious-sounding medical term for the pain caused by cramping that may accompany your period. Cramps are extremely common. When the uterus is working to push out the uterine lining, you may feel cramping. Almost all women experience cramps some of the time, and many women experience them with each cycle. How much discomfort you feel when you menstruate may change over time. So, don't despair. If you have severe cramps, these may lessen as you get older. In addition, cramps can often be relieved by regular exercise, warm baths, laying a hot-water bottle on your belly, or—if they're really bad—an over-the-counter pain reliever like Motrin or Tylenol.

IRREGULAR PERIOD
When you first get your period, you may get it every month like clockwork. But it's possible you will find it's hardly worth keeping track of it because sometimes you get it and sometimes you don't. This is called having an *irregular period*. Many girls who've recently got their period go through this. It usually takes months, and sometimes even a year or two, for your period to become the monthly ritual

that it will be for many years to come. Again, how often your period occurs until it becomes regular is as individual as you are.

AMENORRHEA If you have got your period and then after a year or two you suddenly stop getting it, that's called *amenorrhea,* and it's different from having an irregular period. Amenorrhea may occur because of a hormonal imbalance. It also often occurs among serious athletes whose training regimens are extremely rigorous. And it can occur when a girl is not eating well or is dieting excessively, or both. In general, we could say amenorrhea happens in extreme situations. Those are situations that are very stressful—everything from intensive athletic training or moving to a new house or school to breaking up with your boyfriend or going through your parents' divorce.

If you're in an extreme situation and you stop getting your period, you should talk right away to your mom or dad, or to another adult you trust, and see your doctor. And you should see a doctor if you haven't got your period by the time you are seventeen. Many girls who go through amenorrhea need emotional support as well as physical treatment.

PUTTING THE PIECES TOGETHER

When you start your period, will everything change? No. Will some things change? Yes. You'll have new things to pay attention to. But the sooner you say, "Hey, this is my period and that's the way it's going to be," the better for you. Periods are a natural part of life.

Some girls celebrate with their families and friends when they get their period for the first time. Although you might not want to have a party for a hundred people to announce the news when you get your period, you may want to tell a close friend. On the other hand, you may feel very private about it and decide you don't want to tell anyone but your mother or father. Some girls like to make a note of this big change in their diaries. Whatever your reaction, try to remember that getting your period means you're healthy and moving on into the next stage of your life—adolescence.

Four

What's Going On with Your Emotions

No two kids react to puberty in exactly the same way. Why should they? How each of us feels about the changes we go through is as unique as each individual. In the same way that some aspects of life are harder or easier (like getting up in the morning, doing math homework, reading, saving allowance), so, too, are aspects of puberty more or less difficult for different kids.

NEW THINGS TO WORRY ABOUT

For many of us puberty brings new worries. We may worry because we suddenly feel different from our friends. And, of course, we may worry about our bodies: *Am I too tall—or too short? Are my breasts too small—or too big? When am I going to get my period? Will I be the first one in my class to get it—or the last?* If you find yourself worrying a lot, try to remember that you're not alone. Your friends are going through this, too.

> **"I feel scared about getting my period, and I'm afraid that if people find out, they will tease me. I also think I will be the first in my class to get my period. I do not look forward to it at all."**
> —*Julie, age 11*

> **"I was desperate to get my period from the moment I heard about it when I was nine. I thought it was fascinating and exciting. I just wanted it....I was nearly fifteen when I finally got my period. But I told everyone I had it years before."**
> —*Maria, age 16*

> **"I hate my period. It makes me irritable and mad."**
> —*Ti, age 13*

Why *Do I Have to* Grow Up **?**

Not everyone wants to grow up. Some of us like our lives just the way they are. If you feel this way and you're worried that everything is going to change, it might be comforting to realize that in spite of the physical changes puberty brings, you'll still always be who you are. So try to relax and enjoy your life. And remember, it takes *years* to grow up.

> **"As I get older I want more freedom. I've always been perceived as being older—people on the street ask my friend and I if we're voting."**
> —*Deirdre, age 13*

> **"Sometimes I *do* want to grow up. I see my friends and already they're wearing bras. Sometimes I feel that if I'm not wearing a bra or something, I won't be 'cool.'"** —*Ali, age 11*

> **"I don't want a new load on my back. If being an adult is harder than being a kid, then it has to be pretty tough."**
> —*Amanda, age 11*

How Fast *Can I* Get Through *This* **?**

Some girls want to race through childhood as fast as they can. They can't wait to drive, to date, to make their own decisions. But most of us want to have it both ways: We want to be a kid sometimes and a teenager other times. And why not? Who wants to leave behind a good thing—or at least something you're used to? It can feel like giving up your favorite old shoes. Fortunately, there's room for all these feelings.

HOW PUBERTY AFFECTS YOUR FRIENDSHIPS

When you grow up with a friend, you share something very special—childhood. For as long as you know each other, you can go back in time and reminisce about your third-grade teacher, the mean kid you both hated, tricks you played, your first crushes, and many other things.

Hooray for Friends

As wonderful as it is to have an old friend, one of the great things about life is that we can, and do, make friends throughout our lifetime.

When our bodies go through changes—particularly when they are changing at a different pace than our friends' bodies—we may feel strange. We might even be at the same level of physical development as a good friend but are suddenly interested in different things. In any case, going through puberty, many of us feel private about our bodies, even around our closest friends. But once we grow accustomed to our new bodies, our self-consciousness usually eases.

What *Makes* a **Good** Friend ?

A good friend is someone you can trust. A good friend is someone you can be yourself with, someone who can tell you the truth when you need to know it. A good friend makes you laugh. A good friend is someone who makes your life more joyful.

"I think a good friend has to be funny. How can you have fun with someone who doesn't laugh?"
—*Ali, age 11*

"I know my friends will stand by me—they give me advice when I need it. I know they are there for me."
—*Rebecca, age 14*

"A good friend is someone who you think of as your equal and vice versa. A person who shares feelings, like being scared of puberty."
—*Amanda, age 11*

"A good friend is someone you can trust, talk to, someone who likes some of the same things as you."
—*Libro, age 14*

"A good friend is someone who helps you get through this—and doesn't laugh at you. The girls in my class agreed to wink if we are getting our period. Nobody has winked yet. We also all want to go to the Limited Too or someplace to get bras together."
—*Julie, age 11*

When You Don't Feel Friendly Toward a Friend

Almost all friendships have their ups and downs. This is especially true during puberty. If you find yourself fighting a lot with a friend or feel as if you don't understand each other anymore, hang in there. Chances are you're going to get back together again. Sometimes it just takes time and giving each other a little room. Every relationship goes through tough times.

Tough Times with Friends

Sometimes a fight with a friend can get out of hand. Maybe your close friend has started teasing or excluding you. What can you do now?

Maybe the hardest thing about being teased or made fun of by someone you think of as a close friend is the betrayal of your trust. Betrayal hurts, and even though in most cases you haven't been hurt physically—and in some cases the conflict might result from a misunderstanding—the emotional hurt is real. Never fear. We've all been there. You will get through the pain, and things do get better. But in the meantime, you're suffering and trying to figure out what to do about it.

How to Deal with Your Emotions

◇ Take time to acknowledge what you're feeling. "I am so mad." "I'm so hurt." "I'm so jealous."

◇ Let off steam by: hitting a pillow, going for a walk, exercising, playing a sport.

◇ Talk to a parent, sibling, or trusted adult.

◇ Clear your head; write down your feelings in a journal or notebook. The important thing is to calm down so you can deal with the situation more clearly.

◇ If you've been mean, come clean. It really helps to admit that you've hurt someone. Apologies are wonderful—they can offer you and your friend a fresh start.

The first thing to do is recognize your feelings. And because what you're feeling is painful, it's a good idea to let someone know what's going on, as hard as that may seem. Most of us feel a huge sense of relief when we're able to share our problems with someone we trust. And in times of conflict or confusion, another person's perspective can be very helpful. Together, you and your confidant might come up with ideas that will help you talk to the friend who hurt you.

We know it's hard to confront a friend who has upset you. Most of us aren't used to talking about our feelings—especially angry and jealous feelings. It can be uncomfortable and even scary to do so. This is true no matter how old you are.

Another reason it might be hard to express your feelings is that you're afraid of the consequences. You may think: *If I tell my friend that she hurt or insulted me, she might get angry with me and even stop being my friend.*

Remember, a really good friend is someone who respects and cares about your feelings, just as you respect hers. And if you're brave (it takes courage) and you open up about your feelings, you'll often get really positive results.

It's not mean to tell a friend when you're angry. Here are some ways to go about it:

◉ Find a place where you can have privacy.
◉ Talk to her alone, not in front of other friends.
◉ Think about what you want to say before you get together. You might want to jot down some notes or talk the situation through first with a trusted adult.
◉ Don't start out accusing her. Instead, talk about how you feel.
◉ Give her a chance to talk.
◉ Listen to what she has to say.

Take It Off-line

When you're having a hard time with a friend, it's probably not a good idea to fight by e-mail. For one thing, when you e-mail someone in the heat of an argument you might say something you'll regret and probably don't even mean. And once you've sent an e-mail, it's out there—and it can be forwarded, or copied and pasted, and read by the wrong people. Just what you *don't* want. The other problem with fighting on the Internet is that you can't see your friend's face or hear her voice—so you may be missing some important clues to how she's feeling.

The Sleep on It Rule

If someone sends you an angry e-mail, you might consider waiting until the next day before you respond. Sure, write out your frustrations and save the letter or e-mail. (It's probably easiest to do this on your computer and save the message.) Then the next day, when you're feeling calmer, you can sit down and read what you wrote and see if you still want to send the message. You may discover you have a new perspective on the fight—and on your friendship.

As one of the girls we spoke to said about fighting online: "At least when you're speaking you've got tone. You can tell what each other means by the tone of their voice. Maybe something that's said is just sarcastic. And then you get to respond immediately. When you're e-mailing each other, you can't tell how your friend is *saying* the words. If you're talking on the phone...well, it's instant. You don't have to think, *Well, what do you mean by that?* You can ask."

How You Feel and How You Deal

When you've been hurt or betrayed, you can't help feeling angry. It's normal. You may find yourself thinking mean thoughts. You may even find yourself thinking about how to get revenge. This, too, is normal. So, what do you do when you want to act on those mean feelings? As we've said before, talk to someone you trust. You might want to write down your thoughts in your journal. The point is to find a way to express what you're going through. If you get your feelings out, you'll not only feel better but you won't be so tempted to act mean.

ARE YOU BEING A BULLY?

Take a "bully" quiz from Stop Bullying Now website (www.stopbullyingnow.hrsa.gov). If any of these points describe your behavior, maybe you've been a bully to someone.

1. There's a boy or a girl (or maybe more than one) whom you've repeatedly shoved, or punched or physically pushed around in a mean way just because you felt like it.
2. You had someone else hurt someone you don't like.
3. You've spread a nasty rumor about someone, in conversation, in a note, or through e-mail or instant messaging.
4. You and your friends have regularly kept one or more kids from hanging out or playing with you. Examples: at your lunch table at school, during sports or other activities, or activities that are a part of a club or other kind of group activity.
5. You've teased people in a mean way, calling them names, making fun of their appearance, or the way they talk or dress or act.
6. You've been part of a group that did any of these things— even if you only wanted to be part of the crowd.

Health Resources and Services Administration, U.S. Department of Health and Human Services

What mean Means

- If someone teases you or taunts you,
  that's being mean.
- If someone tells a lie about you, that's mean.
- If someone betrays you by telling a secret
  you've confided in them, that's mean.
- If someone moves away from the lunch table
  when you sit down, that's mean.
- If you walk past a group of kids and find
  they're laughing at you, that's mean.
- In general, anything a friend does to purposely
  upset you and just make you feel bad
  is probably mean.

Bullies

What is a bully? A bully is someone who *repeatedly* tries to hurt another person, either physically or emotionally or both.

Physical bullying is when someone intentionally shoves, trips, or hits you; pulls your hair; or does anything else to hurt you.

Emotional bullying is when someone teases, taunts, calls you names, spreads rumors about you, or gets others to ignore or reject you. Sometimes bullying is nonverbal, which means words are not spoken. In these cases the bully uses gestures, rolls her eyes, makes faces about you to others, or turns her back on you.

94

When a Friend Turns into a Bully

As we mentioned earlier, it's especially painful when someone you think of as a friend turns against you. That's a terrible betrayal. Often the goal of this friend-turned-bully is to have power, to have the upper hand, and one way she can do this is by trying to turn others against you.

If a friend has become a bully, you'll want to tell a parent or a trusted adult as soon as possible. You might try to talk to your friend, but if she doesn't listen to you, then you'll need to distance yourself from her.

How to Cope with a Bully
(Whether She's a Friend or Not)

✳ Talk to a parent, counselor, or trusted teacher. This is *not* something you should deal with alone. If you don't have someone to talk to, call the Girls and Boys Town national hotline (1-800-448-3000). It's free, and someone will be available to talk 24 hours a day.

* Try to avoid situations in which you could be alone with a bully.

* Don't isolate yourself. Try to go places in groups of two or three, but not alone.

* Try to spend time with someone you love. If that person doesn't live nearby, then call or write to that person. A good talk with a good friend can do wonders to boost your spirits.

* Try to find something new to focus on. It could be a sport or theater club, a community service program, or a place where you'll meet new people who share your interests. Look for people who make you laugh or share your sense of humor.

* Many schools have anti-bullying programs. Find out if your school can put one in place. The Empower Program (www.empowerprogram.org) and The Ophelia Project (www.opheliaproject.org) are two organizations that help schools implement anti-bullying programs. The Stop Bullying Now site has antibullying tips for students as well as for parents, teachers, and administrators. Remember, you have the right to be safe!

Bullies on the Internet

Sometimes bullying goes beyond school and into your home via the Internet. If you are the target of hateful e-mails, or instant messaging—or if someone takes a picture of you and posts it without your permission—here are some things you should (or should *not*) do:

* Do not respond by e-mail or any other means. Doing so will only invite more of the same.

- Tell a parent or some other trusted adult. Cyberbullying is hurtful and scary, and you shouldn't deal it with it alone.
- It's a good idea to print out or save hateful e-mails so you can use them as evidence if it comes to that (although we hope it won't—and in most cases it doesn't).
- If you know who's sending you the e-mail, block the address(es).
- Spend some time away from the computer and don't check your e-mail so frequently.
- If anyone threatens to harm you in an e-mail, you *must* tell a parent or some other trusted adult.

LEND a HELPING HAND

What can you do if you see someone being bullied? There are a number of things you can do to help:

- Don't join in the bullying.
- Tell a parent, teacher, school counselor—or some other grown-up you really trust—what's going on.
- Be kind to the kid who's being bullied, if you can. Sit next to her in class or on the bus, include her in an activity, or just give her a friendly smile. Those gestures will help her know she's not alone.
- If you feel it's safe to do so, tell the bully to cut it out.

Staying Safe Online

Just as you wouldn't give strangers your address and phone number, the same common sense should apply when you're online. The main thing you want to remember is to maintain your privacy. Here are some sensible tips to follow:

- Never give your e-mail address to a stranger or to a person you don't know well.
- Find foolproof ways to determine if the person online is who you think he or she is. Have the person relay an experience you've shared or give you an agreed-upon code phrase or word.
- Learn how to block the names attached to e-mails you don't want to receive.
- If anyone acts "weird" to you—for example, if someone writes to you all the time, asks to meet you, asks you to describe yourself physically, or just somehow gives

you the creeps—be honest about how you feel and tell your parents or some other trusted adult.

🌸 When setting up an instant messaging service, protect yourself by not giving out more information than necessary. And *don't* give your address (or any other information about yourself) to anyone online whom you don't know well.

🌸 Be cautious about chat rooms—you don't know the ages or identities of the people you're "chatting" with.

🌸 *Never* agree to meet with any stranger you've chatted with online. You've never met that person, and no matter how well you *think* you know him or her, you simply can't trust someone you've never met.

🌸 It's easy to set up your own chat room with a bunch of friends. Then you've got an online clubhouse of sorts rather than a chat room—and that means you've got an opportunity to really chat.

CELL PHONES AND DIGITAL CAMERAS

More safety tips:

🌸 If you have a digital camera, make sure no one uses it but you.

🌸 Be respectful of others. Don't take embarrassing photos of anyone, even as a joke.

🌸 Never send (or forward) an embarrassing photo to anyone, even a friend, because you don't know where it will end up.

🌸 Don't give out your cell phone number to strangers or people you don't know well.

Rocking the Boat—
The New Kid in Town

Uh-oh. Who's this? No matter how secure and popular we may be, there's a part of all of us that wonders, *How is the new kid in town going to change my life?*

When a new kid comes into our circle of friends, it can feel as if our boat is being rocked—either the boat tips over or everyone has to take a new seat to regain balance. Sometimes the new kid slips into the group and it feels as if you were just waiting for her to arrive. But other times it's threatening, and you worry that the new kid will take *your* place. If you're feeling worried about being "replaced," try talking to a grown-up you trust. Most of us have gone through this kind of thing. Remember, there is no one else like you. Your friends love you for who you are, but that doesn't mean they shouldn't be open to making new friends. It's a good idea for *all* of us to be open—to give new kids a chance.

And yes, we might end up not liking the new kid after all. But then again, maybe we will.

Finding New Friends

Probably all of us have had the wrenching experience of drifting apart from a close friend. Sometimes friendships end abruptly and this can feel like a slap in the face. But however it happens, friendships do change—even break off—and this is part of life.

If you are the one who is leaving behind an old friend, try to go about it kindly. If you are in the position of finding new friends, try to relax—and take your time. Don't be afraid of spending some time alone. You don't have to throw yourself into a new group immediately. Stop and check out the people around you. Try to find someone you sense will be a good friend. Look for kids who enjoy things you are interested in.

One way to meet new people is by trying out a new sport or activity. Putting yourself in an unfamiliar situation is always going to be a little scary, but the scary feeling will pass. Remember, it takes a lot of courage to try new things, but we promise you will gain a lot in return.

What Makes the Cool Kids "Cool"

Often during puberty a girl will move away from her old group into the "cool" group. Cool groups in the past, present, and, most likely, the future have certain things in common: They have an aura, a buzz around them, a magic-circle effect. Typically, the cool kids act superior and aloof. They give the impression that they— *and they alone*—know what is really going on.

COPING WITH "COOL" Remember, "cool" is a kind of invisible armor kids wear. It's a defense, a neat disguise to hide behind. If it's any comfort, remind yourself that inside

> "It's an attitude mostly. Once you're cool, you can do anything you want. The reputation isn't all that delicate. The attitude is, 'I'm in control—everyone listen to me.' The cool kids make others humble."
>
> —Annabel, age 12

> "When you're not in the cool group, you think you're missing out on the time of your life. Then when you're in the cool group for a day, you start to miss your true friends."
>
> —Amanda, age 11

> "It's awful not to be in a cool group. You don't get guys and you are mostly looked down on."
>
> —Veronica, age 14

every cool kid there are as many unanswered questions and insecurities as there are in you. No one—let's repeat that, *no one*—goes through puberty without insecurity. The cool kids are using "cool" as protection.

Very often the cool kids are the ones who have older brothers and sisters. They seem sophisticated and may be more knowledgeable in the ways of the world because of what their siblings have taught them.

> "In my class there isn't really a cool group, but I think that is good because we all play together and that's fun."
>
> —Julie, age 11

> "The cool girls are the sun, and I feel like I'm on Venus."
>
> —Rosie, age 12

Not Everything Changes

Although there *are* lots of changes during puberty, don't forget that not everything changes.

Your bed still has the same cozy pillows and sheets (and stuffed animals or softball mitt). You still have to do your homework (joy or ugh?). You still have your favorite sports, your favorite classes, your favorite CDs.

Your looks change, but you still look like yourself. Your family still loves you and always will. Your friendships go through ups and downs, but deep friendships will last—and if they don't, there will be wonderful new friends to discover.

Entering a new stage of life is like entering a new country. You have to get used to a lot of unfamiliar customs. In this case there are new routines, like taking showers more often, doing more chores around the house, staying up later. Then there are all these new aspects of this new land that just may interest or even fascinate you. But all these changes in your life mean you'll have more on your plate to deal with. This can create stress.

Stress Busters

There are many things you can do to help relieve stress.

YOGA   Some of the postures of yoga can be very helpful in reducing stress, particularly those that focus on your breathing and resting. The "sun salutation" can help you to stretch your body and to relax. The "bow pose" can help to relieve stress in your lower back and massage your abdomen, the "scene of the pain." The "child's pose" can be very comforting and relaxing. In general, yoga can

help you to remember to breathe deeply, because the focus is always on breathing.

DON'T FORGET TO BREATHE
This may sound funny, but many of us don't get enough oxygen. Oh sure, we get enough to stay alive, but in our busy, stressed-out lives we tend to forget to take deep breaths. Instead, many of us take shallow breaths most of the time. So, don't forget to breathe. You might want to try stopping a few times a day to take a few deep breaths. Breathe in deeply, filling your lungs with air. Count to five, then release the breath slowly. Do this about five times, and you're sure to feel a bit better—and feeling a little better can mean a lot.

EXERCISE
As mentioned before, exercise is very important. In fact, just as nothing can ensure your emotional health better than talking it out when you have a problem, nothing ensures your body's health more immediately than exercise. And, oddly enough, exercise can also help you maintain your emotional health. That's because the *endorphins* released into your system when you exercise can raise your endorphin levels and improve your mood. Endorphins are composed of many amino acids that are processed via the pituitary gland. If you are an athlete, you already know this. If you aren't, you can get with the program by simply adding a twenty-minute-or-so walk to your day.

Another idea is to take up a sport, join a team, or take a movement or dance class to get your heart rate going. But if you've got nothing but a jump rope and a some music on hand, you can have as much fun and get as much exercise as anyone, as long as you get off the couch.

"SECURITY BLANKETS" There are days when we all need a coat of armor. It may be because we have too many zits or because it's our first day at a new school or because we're going through tough times at home—whatever the reason, we feel vulnerable. And because we are no longer three years old, we can't drag along our security blankets or stuffed animals to school to help us get through the day—or can we?

On days you're feeling especially sensitive, nervous, or stressed-out, it might help to wear something you love—a pair of earrings your best friend gave you, a favorite baseball hat—or to bring along some silly little windup toy that makes you laugh. We all need security blankets now and then.

Talking It Out

Talking is a great stress buster. It's amazing how relieved we can feel after talking over a problem. Of course, not everyone is comfortable talking about things that bother them, but it's a good idea to at least try.

How Do I Say What I Need To ?

The secret to this is that you just start talking and what you need to say will come. There is no other way. However hard it might be for you to get the conversation going, *get it going*. Once you start talking, you will be surprised at how much easier it is to keep going than it was to start.

TALKING THROUGH WRITING Some people, who are not so comfortable talking, write down their thoughts and concerns, and that makes them feel better. The act of getting something off your chest onto paper can also bring relief.

There are all different ways to try to sort things through. Sometimes we need to write in our journals *and* talk to someone *and* go for a run, shoot some hoops, or listen to music. The more healthful the ways you can help yourself, the better.

TALKING WITH A THERAPIST Everyone goes through tough times, and when we do we often feel depressed or anxious. It's a good idea during these times to talk to someone you trust—a parent, a teacher, an older brother or sister. Sometimes this will do the trick. But often it's helpful to talk to a professional counselor or therapist who is trained to help people sort through their feelings and concerns. You don't have to be feeling desperate to consider getting professional help.

Many of us find that talking to a therapist is almost always

Other Stress-Busting Activities

You may want to try to reduce stress by:

❉ painting

❉ singing

❉ shooting hoops

❉ running

❉ dancing

❉ ice-skating with a friend

❉ swimming

❉ reading a good book, with your favorite blanket over your knees

❉ drinking hot cocoa

❉ listening to music

❉ walking with a friend

❉ lying in a hammock

❉ writing in your journal

And don't forget to exercise.

DeAR Diary,
Today I feel really blue. My best friend is really mad at me and the boy who sits behind me in math is

useful because it can help us understand and cope with our lives. If expense is an issue, there are counselors who will see teens for very little money, or even for free. It's also important to remember that sometimes the first therapist we see isn't the right person for us. Just as we feel more comfortable with different family members or teachers, the same can be true for counselors.

Sometimes when a person is first seeking help and they don't find somebody they like, they give up on the whole idea of therapy. But when you think about it, it really makes much more sense to keep looking until you find the right match for you.

What about Emotional Emergencies?

If a friend tells you she's feeling depressed and then says she's thinking about suicide, *this is an emergency. You must tell an adult you trust right away, no matter what you promised your friend.* Or you can call the Covenant House Nineline at 1-800-999-9999. You may be betraying your friend's confidence, but you might also be saving her life.

Needless to say, if *you're* feeling seriously depressed or suicidal, *you must tell someone you trust right away.* Part of the problem with being depressed is that it often feels like a permanent condition. Everything seems hopeless and impossible. But these feelings are caused by depression, and, if you get help, most likely you'll start to feel better.

ALTERNATIVE MEDICINE

In a lot of ways, the first year during which you have your period is a time of learning *and* a time of adjustment.

Although growing up and getting your period are still not easy, you've got a lot more options than your mother or our mothers did—from the variety of sanitary napkins and tampons you can use to the ways you can deal with premenstrual cramping and other menstrual problems. Apart from traditional Western medicine, there are lots of other ways— which we call *alternative medicine*—you might consider using to make cramps and other side effects of puberty easier to deal with. It is very important that you tell your doctor about what you're doing. What alternative medicine *can* do is to effectively supplement your regular doctor's care.

ACUPUNCTURE   The practice of *acupuncture* originated in China thousands of years ago. In Chinese philosophy, *chi* (or *qi*) is the life energy present in all organisms. This belief extends to Chinese medicine, including acupuncture, which is based on the knowledge that the health of the body is determined by the flow of *chi* through the body. *Chi's* life energy is said to pass through the body through different paths called meridians. There are said to be more than a thousand "acupoints" that can be stimulated to improve the flow of *chi* through the body.

Acupuncture is considered to be particularly effective in treating pain. In this case, we refer to premenstrual and menstrual cramps. For some girls and women, cramps pass in a day, but for others, cramps may be persistent and bother us every month. What you do to relieve your cramps depends on what sort of medicine you and your family believe in. If cramps are a constant problem, acupuncture may be a good way of relieving pain.

When people think of acupuncture, they usually think of the needles used to stimulate points along the meridians. These needles ultimately help people so much that most report they don't even really hurt. If you have an aversion to needles, however, or have seen enough of them already, *acupressure* may be a better alternative for you.

Acupressure is a therapy that utilizes the same spots on the meridians in the body that affect the flow of *chi,* but it does not involve the use of needles. Instead, it is a massage technique, based on the same philosophy as acupuncture, that can help to relieve your physical discomfort.

CHIROPRACTIC TREATMENT *Chiropractic medicine* is based on the physical relationship between the spinal column and the rest of the body, particularly the muscles and bones that support the nervous system. The concept behind chiropractic is that the spinal column acts as a chart that instructs the nervous system.

A chiropractic treatment may relieve menstrual cramping and the lower-back pain that often accompanies menstruation for some girls. For other girls, such treatment may have no effect.

A decade or two ago, chiropractors were associated with some very scary ideas and words. Common misnomers were used by many who did not understand the discipline. People referred to "cracking" the back or neck (ugh!) and "popping" a joint back into place. How can you "pop" a joint? Well, you can't, nor can you "crack" a back. Doing so would cause major injuries, the kinds of problems that chiropractic manipulation strives to correct. As our understanding of chiropractic medicine has grown, negative terms and practices have pretty much dropped from use. You can be assured, there is nothing scary or weird about seeing a chiropractor, and the treatment you receive may bring you real relief.

REFLEXOLOGY

Reflexology is based on the concept that there are reflex areas in the hands and feet that trigger responses in every part of the body, including the organs and glands. Though many traditional doctors argue with this, those who use reflexology believe it helps to reduce tensions and relieve stress. Reflexology may also improve your blood supply and can result in deep relaxation.

A reflexologist will use precise pressure on the feet or hands to eliminate blockages of what they refer to as the energy flow. This makes at least a certain amount of sense because there are about 7,200 nerve endings in each of your feet. We use our feet a lot. We take them for granted. Our soles pound away on pavement, gym floors, and stairs. And we rarely pamper them. Imagine how good you might feel when these nerve endings are well cared for.

If you do choose to go to a reflexologist around the time your period is due, remember to detail for her or him what your symptoms are, particularly where you are feeling pain. This information will help the reflexologist pinpoint your problem. If nothing else, you and your feet and hands will find this a pleasurable experience.

HERBAL MEDICINE   *Herbal medicines* have been around for thousands of years in one form or another. We might not realize it, but many of us take advantage of herbal medicine every day. When we drink a cup of herbal tea, we're using a form of herbal medicine. Approximately a quarter of all prescription drugs have been derived from herbs, shrubs, or trees.

Not all herbs are good for you, however. It's very important to use the herbs available on the market with care. Not all of them are safe. You should never ingest an herb without telling your doctor, the nurse at school, or another adult you trust that you are doing so. Some herbs have side effects and/or can make you sick, and if you are taking other medications, the combination could be dangerous to your health. It's also a good idea to start with a very small test dose, if you do take an herb, just to make sure you are not allergic.

HOMEOPATHY

The core belief of *homeopathy* is that "like cures like." This idea is reflected in the way immunization works. When you are vaccinated with a shot to protect you from getting chicken pox, the flu, or another illness, you are actually being given a small amount of the virus that causes the illness. Because the amount is small enough, you don't actually get sick. Instead, your body's immune system develops the antibodies that fight the illness, and this protects you should you ever be exposed to the illness again.

In homeopathic medicine, a person with a fever will take a type of medicine that would cause a fever in a healthy person. Taking tiny amounts of medicine helps the body fight the disease and helps the person get well. Today there are medical doctors who call themselves homeopathic doctors; they treat all illnesses homeopathically before they turn to using traditional medicine.

Those who follow homeopathy believe it can help with almost any medical problem, including menstrual cramps. If your cramps are severe, or if you have trouble sleeping and other remedies you've tried haven't worked, you might want to consider, with your family, homeopathy.

VITAMIN THERAPY

Taking vitamins is important, but it's more important to get the nutrients you need from the food you eat. *Don't think of a vitamin as a substitute for food.* Vitamins can supplement your diet but should not serve as a replacement for nutritious food.

Once you reach age twelve or thirteen, you might consider taking a calcium supplement. Ask your doctor or your nurse what the right amount for you to take is. Calcium is essential for keeping our bones healthy and strong. It is especially important for women, because as women age, our bones become more brittle. Also, as already mentioned, calcium can help reduce the symptoms of PMS.

There are no vitamin supplements known to actually relieve menstrual cramps, but taking a multivitamin regularly can help keep you healthy. Staying healthy will help to minimize cramps. Just think of how much worse you feel when you're tired, draggy, and under the weather, and then you get your period! The better you feel, the less you'll be bothered by cramps and other menstrual symptoms.

THERAPEUTIC MASSAGE *Massage* is good for the body, whether or not it has any further medicinal value. Certainly, your muscles tense up when you are about to get your period, and massage can relax those tight muscles and the tension they cause.

If your mom or dad or another family member thinks massage is cool, then you've got it made. They probably know a masseuse who'll give you a great massage. If not, or if your parents think massage is too expensive, wooden massage aids, which you can use on yourself, are available at most health food stores. Also, your own strong hands can massage away the tension in your shoulders and your lower back any old time.

YOGA   *Yoga* is both a spiritual and a physical discipline. It increases the flexibility of your joints and muscles, and can improve your health by teaching you to breathe more deeply. If you are having menstrual cramps and feeling tension prior to your period, yoga can be particularly helpful in releasing that tension and calming you. That's why some people say yoga is for the mind as well as the body. It can help you learn to relax and to shift your focus away from whatever tension or pain you may be experiencing. Breathing and relaxation exercises, stretching, and balancing poses can help to relieve cramps and to improve your state of mind. Yoga's ability to ease tension may stand you in good stead for all of your life.

AROMATHERAPY   There have been no studies that prove that *aromatherapy* has any lasting medical value. However, it's nice to surround yourself with pleasant scents in a world that has some very bad smells. It's also true that good scents can make you feel calmer. Just think about how you feel when you smell a favorite flower.

Many ordinary drugstores and most health food stores carry aromatherapy products for skin and bathing, as well as mists for your face and candles and sprays for your home. Whatever the medicinal value, the main thing about aromatherapy is that it can soothe you and help you to feel better when you're not feeling so great.

Here are some simple, inexpensive ways to include aromatherapy in your life:

- Use a washcloth, a pair of massage gloves (available in drugstores and health food stores), or your bare hands to massage an aromatherapy oil into your skin. Just as massage therapy can help to relax your muscles and your mind, this will, too—and it will make you smell great.
- Take a bath using aromatherapy bath oil. Many inexpensive soothing scents are available.
- Spray your room with a spray whose smell you especially like. You can find sprays with names like Energy, Balance, Joy, and Rejuvenation.
- Breathe in an aroma nose therapy (make sure you pick a mild scent made for the nose!) to give yourself a head start on a tough day.
- Burn an aromatherapy candle while you're doing homework, but make sure it cannot light anything on fire. Never leave a burning candle unattended, and always be sure to blow it out!

Talk to Your Doctor First

As previously noted, you should discuss with your regular doctor anything you plan to do outside of traditional medical treatment. If you suffer from diabetes or have other health complications, you should be particularly careful to inform your doctor about any alternative medicine you think might help you through puberty.

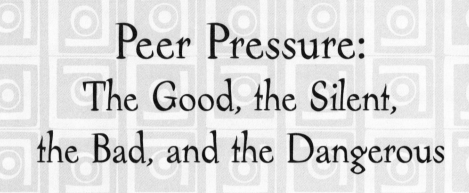

Five

Peer Pressure: The Good, the Silent, the Bad, and the Dangerous

*W*e love our friends for better or for worse, but that does not necessarily mean we should always trust their advice. At one time or another we've all felt pressured or influenced by our friends or classmates to do something or to act in a certain way. This isn't always a bad thing. But it isn't always a good thing, either.

Good Peer Pressure

All your friends are taking tap dancing. You want to try it, but you fear that you're a hopeless klutz. Your friends encourage you to take the class with them. They really, really want you to come, too, and they let you know it. That's *positive peer pressure*. Your friends are trying something new—and attempting to persuade you to try something new, too.

Silent Peer Pressure

Almost everyone you know is wearing a certain style or brand of sneaker. No one has said that you *must* wear this kind of sneaker, but you'd feel out of the fashion loop if you didn't. So you do. That's *silent*, or unspoken, *peer pressure*.

Bad Peer Pressure

You're invited to a birthday slumber party. During the party the birthday girl happily announces that she's rented a whole bunch of horror movies. You *hate* horror movies. You find them violent and disturbing. The scary movie you saw a few years ago *still* comes back to haunt you. You work up the courage to say you're not a big fan of scary movies, so maybe you'll slip into the other room and read or do something else while the movies are on.

"*Come on,*" a girl says. "These are great movies. Sure they're scary, but that's the fun part!"

You hesitate. Some of the other kids act impatient with you. They think you're being a baby *and* a drag. What's the big deal, anyway?

This is *bad*, or negative, *peer pressure*. Why? Because you're being pressured to do something that makes you very

uncomfortable. Listen to your gut feelings. You're being pressured to do something you know will have negative consequences on your life, even though it probably won't ruin it. The last time you saw a scary movie you had horrible nightmares and you were afraid to be alone in the house for a month. And if you have only one sleepless night—well, that's bad enough right there.

Dangerous Peer Pressure

You're at a party having a so-so time when an older boy you've had a secret crush on for the past year suddenly asks you to dance. He's charismatic and handsome, and it's really exciting to dance with him. You spend the rest of the night talking and dancing together. He asks if he can drive you home, but you're worried because he's been drinking beer. You tell him you're not sure it's a good idea for him to drive. He says not to be silly—he's driven plenty of times when he's had much more to drink than he has now. "Believe me," he tells you, "I know my limit."

This is *dangerous peer pressure* because someone is trying to get you to do something potentially life threatening, such as getting into a car with a driver who's been drinking. Other forms of dangerous peer pressure include someone trying to get you to take drugs and someone pressuring you to have sex—especially unprotected sex.

RESISTING PEER PRESSURE

So, how do we resist peer pressure and stand up for ourselves when we need to? Unfortunately, sometimes saying no isn't easy. This is true for adults as well as for kids. But why can it be so hard to say no? There are lots of reasons, including because:

- You might lose a friend or the person you're romantically involved with if you don't give in.
- Going along with the group is easier than having a fight.
- You're afraid of being rejected, laughed at, or left out.
- You don't have enough time to think it through.
- You're curious and what you're being asked to do just might be fun.
- You're afraid of what will happen if you say no.
- You haven't had enough practice saying no.

Yes, it's hard to say no, but there are some reasons that might make doing so easier. You say no because:

- You're being asked to do something that could damage your health.
- You could be hurt, physically and/or emotionally.
- You could hurt a good friend.
- You could lose your parents' trust.
- *You don't want to!*

How Can I Resist Caving in to Peer Pressure?

Practice, practice, practice.

Practice with friends, parents, or other adults you trust how you might handle a difficult situation. This playacting might seem silly at first, but if you think about it, *most* things people do in life take practice. An actor doesn't perform on opening night without lots of rehearsals. A dancer doesn't leap onto the stage without hours of warm-ups. And a lawyer doesn't make her case to the jury without researching and rehearsing what she's going to say.

Rehearsing prepares us, and being prepared gives us more confidence. And though we certainly can't predict what's going to happen in every new situation, we can practice a few lines and strategies that might help us. One way of being prepared is to always have a backup plan with your parents or another grown-up you trust. Talk to your parents about how to structure this.

Learning to Stand Up for Yourself

Whether you're naturally shy, or even if you're naturally outspoken, you could probably use some tips that will help you to stand up for yourself. For starters, you may need to remind yourself that just as your body belongs to you and you alone, so do your thoughts and feelings. Your feelings are yours, *period*. Nobody can tell you what to feel. If someone is pressuring you to do something and it feels wrong, you have every right to say so.

Be Assertive, Not Aggressive

In every situation there is a goal and an outcome, and they're not always the same. Sometimes we have a goal, but we don't do what we need to do to get there. It helps to think about what result you want *before* you make a move. Think about the outcome. What is it you want and how do you want the situation to end? Probably not in a big fight. The best way to go about this is to state your feelings as clearly as possible but without an attitude. This is called *being assertive*.

If you are too pushy or insulting or threatening, either verbally or physically, you will only make the other person angry. This is called *being aggressive*. If you are aggressive, it's much harder to get what you really want. For example, let's say someone is pressuring you to drink alcohol. Assertive responses

might be: "I don't drink because it makes me sick," or "I don't drink because I don't want to get drunk," or "I don't like the taste," or "Drinking is not for me." Aggressive responses might be something like: "Just because you like being a drunken fool doesn't mean I do," or "Quit being such an idiot."

But let's say you're in a situation where nobody is listening to what you say, no one seems to care what you feel, or you don't feel like explaining yourself. Well, you don't have to. This is especially true when someone wants you to do something unsafe. Feel free to say, "I gotta go."

You certainly don't need to explain yourself, but if you'd feel more comfortable giving an excuse, go ahead. You can always say you have another commitment, like walking the dog, baby-sitting, or going to your piano lesson. The point is to escape the situation. Later on you may want to ask yourself whether you want to be friends with someone who encourages you to do something unsafe.

It can be hard to say no. But with practice it does become a little easier. Remember that you won't be able to stand up for yourself or voice your true feelings in *every* situation. *And it's very important not to be hard on yourself if you can't always succeed.* You are still young and you are still learning about life. And life always involves taking a few steps forward and a few steps backward. Life is about making mistakes. And it's about learning from our mistakes.

Six

Protecting Yourself

What is intuition? *Intuition* means to know something without having consciously learned it. Intuition is the gut reaction we have that tells us something is important. Like a cat's whiskers, our intuition warns us when a situation or a person is threatening or dangerous.

These gut feelings come over us quickly and often cause our hearts to race or give us that butterflies-in-the-stomach sensation. These gut reactions tell us things like: "There's something weird about this person," or "This subway station feels creepy," or "Something feels odd here," or "Something seems wrong."

Trusting Your Instincts

All of us have been in situations where we've felt flashes of fear or uneasiness. And like Snow White in the fairy tale, we don't always pay attention to these feelings. Even though she doesn't feel right about it, Snow White goes ahead and takes a bite out of that famous poison apple. And because it's a fairy tale, her handsome prince arrives to save her.

But what was Snow White's mistake in the first place? She didn't trust her gut reaction, fear. She didn't *know* the old beggar woman selling apples was really her wicked stepmother. And yet, something inside Snow White said, *"Beware of this woman."* If Snow White were a dog, she'd have barked at the old woman, or maybe bit her.

But people don't always pay attention to their gut reactions the way animals do. And we want to tell you how important it is to trust your instincts.

HOW TO BE SAFE BUT NOT FEARFUL

You don't want to go out into the world as a cowering, nervous wreck, suspecting that every stranger you pass is out to get you. We don't want you to, either. You can't enjoy anything if you're scared all the time. And the point is to enjoy everything you can. We want you to go into the world with a sense of excitement and curiosity. To do this, you need to be cautious and keep your wits about you, but you need not be fearful.

Think of figuring out how to protect yourself as another learning experience. As you begin to travel through this world on your own, you need to know the various techniques for dealing with danger, just as you need to know your math and how to read and how to do all the other things you've been studying.

So here are some tips that can help you to protect yourself as you get to know this rich, rewarding, and sometimes— just sometimes—scary world.

Know What to Look Out For

It's a good idea to talk with your parents about when you need to be extra cautious or wary. In general, you should be uneasy if:

128

- a stranger starts talking to you from his (or her) car
- a stranger approaches you—whether you are on the street, in a mall, or at a park—and starts acting very friendly
- a man or an older boy you don't know or don't know *well* asks you to go for a ride with him, or asks you to go to his house
- a stranger wants to take your picture or asks you to be in a movie

Self-Defense

One of the best things you can do is to take a self-defense class. It may make you more confident and could help you in a dangerous situation.

HOW TO KEEP SAFE

⊠ Be aware of what's going on around you.

⊠ Always let someone know where you are going and when you'll be back.

⊠ Be honest about telling people about your plans—doing so could save your life, or at least save others (like your parents) from a lot of worry.

⊠ Try to go places in groups of two or three, not alone.

⊠ Don't talk to strangers.

⊠ Don't assume you know someone just because you've seen him around and because he seems nice. An acquaintance is someone you don't know well and should not necessarily trust.

⊠ Don't hang out in abandoned buildings or a part of the park where few people go.

⊠ Don't go walking, blading, or riding down deserted paths or roads; always try to be where people can see, hear, and help you if necessary.

⊠ Never go anywhere with a stranger or anyone you don't know well.

If anyone threatens you or tries to grab you, make as much noise as possible—scream for help, kick, pretend to vomit. Think of yourself as a fire alarm and do anything you can to cause a scene, alert other people, and frighten off your attacker.

When You're Home Alone

Talk to your parents about how to be safe when you're home alone. Have a plan in place in case of fire, blackouts, earthquakes, and other emergencies. It's a good idea to review these plans every year. Make sure you understand what to do, where to go, whom to call. Remember:

- Be sure you always have flashlights, batteries, and candles in the house.

- Keep a list of important phone numbers by the phone. Always have a number on hand where you can reach your parents or another trusted adult.

- Keep all doors locked, as well as first-floor windows.

- Keep curtains or shades closed at night, so no one can see inside your house.

- Never open the door without looking to see who's there. (If you can look from a window, even better.) *If it's not someone you're expecting, don't open the door.*

- When you are home alone, tell callers that your parents are unavailable to come to the phone.

- If you feel uneasy about anything when you're on your own, call your parents or a trusted adult.

What Would **YOU** Do in These Situations?

1. You and your girlfriend are sitting in a movie theater. A man comes and sits right next to you even though there are *lots* of empty seats to choose from. You get a creepy feeling from him, but you are not sure why. You'd like to move, but you're afraid he might *know* you are moving away from him and get mad. What should you do?

Move to a new seat. Why? Because a grown man should not come and sit next to young girls or boys when there are many other places for him to sit. Although he may be harmless, always feel free to move just because you want to. Remember, that little flash of uneasiness you experienced when he sat down next to you could have been a warning: *Something is not right here.*

2. You are waiting for the elevator at the mall parking lot. The elevator arrives and there's a group of teenage boys in it. Suddenly you feel nervous. You hesitate about getting in. The fact is, you don't want to get into the elevator. What should you do?

Wait for another elevator. You don't have to get into an elevator with strangers who make you uneasy. If a tiny voice inside you is saying, "I'm not comfortable with this," listen to that voice. You don't need a long list of reasons for your decision. Sometimes all we get from a stranger is a weird feeling, but that's enough. Trusting this feeling is how we protect ourselves from potential danger.

3. You are walking to the bus stop alone and a nice-looking, friendly young man starts talking to you. He compliments

you, remarking on how pretty you are. Before you know it, he's walking along beside you, making conversation the whole time. He asks how old you are, who you live with, where you are coming from, and where you are going. He seems like such a nice guy that before you realize it, you are answering his questions. But when he tells you he'd like to get together and he asks for your phone number, something makes you uneasy, so you don't give it to him. You are relieved when the bus comes. This whole incident leaves you with a creepy feeling. You're worried you'll see the same young man again and that he'll start following you. You wonder how else you could have handled the situation. Here are some ideas:

Don't let a stranger draw you into a conversation. Remember that no matter how nice he (or she) may seem, a stranger is someone you don't know and therefore cannot trust.

Cut off the conversation. Simply say, "I don't talk to strangers." If he (or she) persists, put up your hand and say, "Stop," or "Back off," or "Leave me alone," or "Go away." Okay, if he's a really bad guy, he's probably not going to leave just because you said, "Go away." One girl we talked to pretended to throw up, and the man who was bothering her left. Another girl acted "crazy," waving her arms and talking baby talk, and the man went away. However you do it, your goal is to get away from the person who is bothering you as safely and as quickly as you can.

If the stranger persists, go into a store and call an adult you trust to come to get you. If there's no store, ring a doorbell or ask a doorman, guard, or another adult nearby for help. If you see that the stranger is following you, don't be afraid to run. And if you can't find someone to help, call the police. Always tell your parents about the incident.

Seven

What You Never Wanted Anyone to Know You Want to Know about Sex

For many kids, *sex* is the biggest cringe word of them all. If you think the whole idea of sex is gross, hilariously funny, unbelievable, or just plain weird, you're not alone. Most of us have those feelings when we're young. Nobody understands sex right away. The idea, for now, is to get the basic facts. As you grow older you can take in more information, bit by bit.

The word *sex* has more than one meaning. It can mean the sex of a person, as in male or female. It can also refer to having sex, or "coitus" as they say in the medical books. When people talk about having sex, they usually mean having sexual intercourse, but they may be referring to other sexual activities as well, including everything from making out to oral or anal sex.

THE PRELUDE TO SEX

Before actually having sexual intercourse, a couple engages in what is sometimes called *foreplay*. This usually begins when two people are fully or almost fully clothed and leads to partial or complete undressing. Foreplay includes cuddling, hugging, and kissing, which helps each person become aroused. It can also include talking and telling each other how you feel. Caressing and kissing the breasts, and touching each other's genitals, can also be part of foreplay. When the man is sexually stimulated, his penis will become erect and stiff. This is called having an *erection*. A penis gets larger when it is erect. There may be some fluid at the tip. This is due to the release of just a few drops of semen at the time of erection, and the fluid lubricates the penis, making it easier to insert into the vagina. As the woman becomes aroused, her vagina becomes wet and slippery. When the penis is erect and the woman is aroused, it is possible for the man to insert his penis into the woman's vagina, and to begin intercourse.

During sexual intercourse the man and the woman move their bodies together, and they develop a rhythm of pushing back and forth that is very natural and exciting for both people. This feeling of excitement often leads to having an *orgasm,* which is also called *climaxing.* An orgasm is a feeling of intense pleasure. When a man has an orgasm, his penis *ejaculates,* or releases semen, into the woman's vagina. For a woman an orgasm can come at almost any time during sex, and along with the feeling of intense pleasure, she may also feel moist or

135

wet in her vagina. Her partner may also stimulate her clitoris and genital area with his hands or mouth to bring her to orgasm. This is how most women find it easiest to have an orgasm. A woman may have more than one orgasm during intercourse, or a woman might not have an orgasm but still find the experience pleasurable. Nature created sexual intercourse to be a pleasurable experience because this is how the next generation comes to be.

How Does a Woman Become Pregnant?

In order for a pregnancy to occur, two things must take place: fertilization and implantation. This is how the whole thing works:

1. The ovary releases an egg.
2. The egg travels into the fallopian tube.
3. If the egg meets a sperm, they combine and the egg is fertilized. This is called *fertilization.*
4. The fertilized egg travels through the fallopian tube to the uterus.
5. The fertilized egg implants itself in the lining of the uterus, like a tree setting down roots in soil. This is called *implantation.*
6. During *pregnancy,* for approximately the next nine months, the tiny implanted egg will develop into an embryo and then a fetus. All the while, it's being housed in the woman's womb and nourished by nature's ingenious system of transferring nutrients from the woman's blood to the growing fetus through its umbilical cord.

How Are Twins Made?

Fraternal twins occur when two eggs are fertilized by two sperm. They may be the same sex or different sexes.
Identical twins occur when one egg is fertilized by one sperm and splits into two individual balls of cells after fertilization. These twins are always the same sex.
Conjoined twins occur when identical twins fail to separate completely and are instead joined together by a specific body part.

MAKING LOVE

Most young kids think the *only* reason adults have sex is to make a baby. That is certainly one reason. But many people have sex because it's a physical way to show their love for each other. This is why sex is also referred to as *making love*. It's important to know that sex affects our feelings as much as our bodies. Ideally, having sex with someone you love and trust is a positive experience, physically and emotionally, and even spiritually.

Common Questions about Sex

Why is an erect penis sometimes called a boner?

When a penis is erect, it may feel as hard as a bone. But there are no bones in the penis. When a male is sexually aroused, his penis—made up of spongy tissue—fills with blood, making the penis hard and causing it to stick out.

Can a first grader get an erection?

Yes. Males of all ages get erections, including baby boys. Males may have an erection when their bladder is full. And they may get an erection for no apparent reason at all. Sometimes erections are caused by sexy feelings and sometimes they are not. Having erections is a normal part of being male.

What is a "wet dream"?

When a male ejaculates, or releases semen, while sleeping, this is called a *wet dream* or a *nocturnal emission.* This is a normal way for a male body to release the sperm that is produced in the testicles.

Are sperm and semen the same thing?

No. Semen is made up of about 5 percent sperm. The remaining 95 percent of the fluid is from the prostate gland and the seminal vesicles, and is mostly sugars and proteins.

When a male ejaculates, how much fluid comes out?

There's about one to three teaspoons of fluid in an ejaculation. The fluid is usually cloudy and white, but sometimes it might be yellowish or grayish.

How many sperm are released in one ejaculation?

There are about 200 to 300 million sperm in one ejaculation.

Can more than one sperm enter an egg?

No, because as soon as one sperm enters an egg, the egg forms a shield that prevents any other sperm from getting in.

Why do sperm have tails?

So they can swim. Remember, the mission of the sperm is to fertilize the woman's egg. This means sperm have to get to the egg when it's in the woman's fallopian tube, because this is the place where fertilization takes place.

To get there, the sperm, which look like tadpoles, must swim up the vagina, past the cervix and through the uterus, to a fallopian tube. Most sperm don't complete the journey because they are very fragile.

Which direction do the sperm swim in?

All directions.

Which is bigger, the sperm or the egg?

The egg is more than a hundred times bigger than the sperm. The egg is about the size of a grain of sand. Sperm are so tiny you need a microscope to see them.

How long do sperm live?

Sperm can live up to ten days, although most live only three to five. It's possible for a woman to get pregnant a whole week *after* she's had intercourse. If any sperm remain alive that long, her egg could meet a seven- to ten-day-old sperm.

How long does an egg live?

Twenty-four hours.

Because a girl is born with all her eggs, can she get pregnant when she's a baby?

No. Although a girl is born with all her eggs, she does not start *ovulating,* or releasing eggs, until she enters puberty.

If a pregnant woman has sex, can she get pregnant again?

No, because while she's pregnant, a woman stops ovulating. This means she doesn't release any eggs. Women do not get their period when they are pregnant because the uterus is using the lining it would otherwise shed every month.

Why do females have two ovaries and males have two testicles?

So that if one isn't working there's a spare.

What does *menopause* mean?

This is the time when women stop ovulating, or releasing eggs, usually around age fifty.

Does everyone reproduce?

No. Some people aren't able to have children and they choose to adopt. And some people decide not to have children simply because they don't want to be a parent. This doesn't necessarily mean they don't like kids. Many people who enjoy working with kids (teachers and pediatricians, among others) may still decide not to raise a family of their own. Life is full of choices. Whatever choices people make are the ones that are right for them.

Looking for Love

In order to have a healthy, loving relationship with someone, we have to pick a respectful and loving partner. As we grow we learn who these people are. But this takes time.

Our friend Ivy always asks the girls in her health education classes what kind of characteristics they might look for in a potential partner or future husband. Here are some of their answers:

- ♥ a sense of humor
- ♥ honesty
- ♥ kindness
- ♥ someone with shared interests
- ♥ someone smart who can deal with stuff
- ♥ someone who knows right from wrong
- ♥ someone who is respectful
- ♥ someone who is fun
- ♥ someone who is trustworthy

Ivy always tells her students, "You deserve nothing less than *everything* that is on that list!" We agree. We think it's far better to hang out with your friends and spend time on your own than to have a romantic relationship with someone who doesn't give you the love and respect you deserve!

There are also certain characteristics in a partner that should send you running the other way. If your boyfriend ever demonstrates a violent temper, hits or pushes you, or is consistently mean to you, these are signs that you should end the relationship.

Friendship & Sex

When you contemplate a subject as vast as sex, it is important to remember this fact: The healthiest sexual relationships are based on friendship first. Whenever you feel pressured to rush or catch up sexually, remembering this fact can help you realize that going slow is best.

WAITING TILL YOU'RE OLDER

People have sex to express their love, and people have sex because they want to have children, and people have sex because it feels good, but unfortunately, some people (particularly girls) have sex because they think they are *supposed* to. We want you to know that no one is *supposed* to have sex; it's your personal choice.

As we said before, sex affects our feelings as much as our bodies. It should involve being with a person who is respectful, loving, and trustworthy. It is hard to put all these necessary pieces together (the feelings, the trust, the right person) at a young age—all the more reason for not having sex until you are grown up.

Why Would a Girl Have Sex Before She's Ready?

There are lots of reasons a girl might have sex too soon, including because:

SEX IS NOT A GAME

Some guys think of having sex as winning a trophy. Well, it's not. It's an act that carries a lot of responsibility with it. No one should pressure herself (or himself) to have sex.

- ✳ she's insecure
- ✳ she feels pressure from her friends
- ✳ she thinks it will make her more grown-up
- ✳ she views sex as a way to get back at her parents
- ✳ she's lonely
- ✳ she thinks it will make her boyfriend love her
- ✳ she's afraid her boyfriend will leave her if she doesn't
- ✳ her boyfriend tells her she should
- ✳ she's forced to

Who Are You Attracted To?

What do *gay, straight,* and *bi* mean? *Gay,* or *homosexual,* means you're attracted to people who are the same sex as you are. Men who are homosexuals are often called gay. Women who are homosexuals are called gay or *lesbian*. People who are attracted to people of the opposite sex are called straight or *heterosexual*. People who are attracted to both sexes are called bi, or *bisexual*.

Here's the deal. Being confused by sex, being afraid of sex, and having sexual desires are all normal when you face this big topic. It's important to understand that sexual feelings and attractions are not always clear-cut. Adolescence is a time during which you face enormous changes. They don't happen all at once and they don't happen neatly. You might feel attracted to your best girlfriend, when you're perfectly happy dating your boyfriend. You might have a fight with your boyfriend and be attracted to another boy or girl. Don't worry about conflicting sexual feelings. They happen to everyone. It's important to remember that you don't have to:

◉ be embarrassed by your feelings
◉ be threatened by your feelings
◉ act on your feelings

During adolescence your sexual identity is in flux. It's normal to have sexual feelings that are directed at both boys and girls. Although some teens are sure they are straight or gay, others are not. Just as you don't have to be in a hurry to grow up, you also don't have to rush to decide whom you are attracted to or even whether you're attracted to males or females.

Although it's normal and part of nature to be straight, gay, or bi, many people in our society are fearful and prejudiced against people who are not straight. This can make it very difficult for a gay person to feel comfortable about being gay. And because gay people are sometimes attacked verbally and physically, a gay person may be afraid to be openly gay.

Thankfully, there are gay organizations all over the country that can help gay and bi teens find the support they may need. There are also support groups for friends and parents of gays and bi teens. For information on organizations that support gay or questioning youth, contact the National Youth Advocacy Coalition (NYAC) at 1-800-541-6922 or 202-319-9513 (TTY for the hearing impaired.)

Remember, our sexual orientation (which sex we're attracted to) is just one part of who we are. It's very important that we don't judge people by their sexual orientation. Whether we are gay, straight, or bi, we are all equally human and should treat one another with respect and dignity.

If I Have a Crush on a Girl, Am I Gay?

Lots of kids go through stages during which they are attracted to people of the same sex, but it doesn't necessarily mean they are gay.

Remember that there are different kinds of love. Not all types of love are romantic or sexual. Sometimes you might feel like you love someone because you admire or respect him or her.

Sex and Health

There are a number of ways that sex can affect your health, both physically and emotionally. This is why it's a good idea for young people to wait until they are grown-up and mature enough to understand and handle these risks.

How Can I Resist Sexual Pressure?

Your body is your own. Only you get to decide what to do with it. It is *disrespectful and wrong* for anyone to pressure another person into kissing, hugging, touching, or intercourse. Having sex should *never* be a one-sided situation, where one person wants to and the other doesn't.

Often a girl may not want to have sex but still has trouble resisting sexual pressure. Learning to resist sexual pressure takes *practice*. A good health education class will give you some techniques for saying no. Still, it's not always an easy thing to do.

On the next page are a few examples of effective responses to sexual pressure, from an organization called Girls Incorporated, which teaches girls skills to resist such advances:

Boy says:	"Everybody's doing it."
Girl responds:	"Well, I'm not everybody—I'm me. Besides, I know it's not true that everybody's doing it."
Boy says:	"If you love me, you'll have sex with me."
Girl responds:	"If you love me, you'll respect my feelings and not push me into something I'm not ready for."
Boy says:	"We've had sex before, so what's the problem now?"
Girl responds:	"I have a right to change my mind. I've decided to wait until I'm older to have sex again."

THE RIGHT TO CHANGE YOUR MIND

This is a very important idea. It would be impossible to go through life without rethinking some decisions we've made. If we can change our mind about keeping our hair long or cutting it short, why can't we change our mind about something as important as sex? So remember, just because a person has had sex in the past doesn't mean she or he has to keep on having sex.

Physical Ways Sex Can Affect Your Health

* Unwanted pregnancy
* STDs *(sexually transmitted diseases)*, including HIV
* Infections, such as bladder or yeast infections

We must tell you that it's very difficult for adults to cope with unwanted pregnancies and certain STDs, including HIV, but coping with these problems is even harder for teens.

Emotional Ways Sex Can Affect Your Health

* Having sex before she's ready can make a girl feel vulnerable and unhappy.
* Having sex with the wrong person can be a miserable experience that can linger in a girl's memory for a long time.
* Most girls who have sex when they're young wish they had waited until they were older.
* Having sex before a girl is ready can make her feel hurt, guilty, ashamed, angry, and depressed.

Don't Be Afraid to Ask

What Is Masturbation?

Just as our ears are sensitive to sound and our eyes sensitive to light, our sex organs are sensitive to touch. This is true because there are many nerve endings in the clitoris and the penis. Other parts of our bodies are also sensitive to touch, such as our ears, our necks, and our breasts.

We think masturbation is a rather cold and harsh-sounding word for something that many people find very pleasurable and comforting. Masturbation is also called playing with yourself, which doesn't sound much better, in our opinion. Masturbation is when a person touches her or his genitals in a way that feels good.

What Is an Orgasm?

When people masturbate or have intercourse, they may have an orgasm (also called coming or climaxing), which is an intense feeling of physical pleasure. When a girl has an orgasm, she may feel moist or wet in her vaginal area. When a boy has an orgasm, he ejaculates, or releases semen. Often people masturbate because they want to have an orgasm. This is because an orgasm can bring not only a feeling of pleasure but also a feeling of release, followed by a sense of relief and relaxation. For many people, being able to achieve an orgasm takes practice. And that's just fine.

So, It's Normal to Masturbate?

Certainly. Just as it's normal to have sexual feelings and desires (remember, we are all sexual beings), it's also normal to want to touch one's own body for the simple reason that it feels good. After all, your body belongs to you, and if you enjoy touching it, that's your right. It's a good idea to make sure your hands are clean and to masturbate in private, because it's a special, private kind of experience.

Is It Normal Not to Masturbate?

Of course. Everyone is different, and not everybody chooses to masturbate. Some people don't because it goes against their religious beliefs. Some people choose not to because they don't have any desire. But some people choose not to masturbate because they've been told it's "dirty." It's not.

What Is Oral Sex?

Oral sex is stimulating the genitals with the mouth, either on the vulva or the penis.

What Is Anal Sex?

Anal sex involves a male putting his penis into the anus of either another male or a female. Unfortunately, some girls and women think that by having anal sex they're protecting themselves from getting pregnant. But it is possible to get pregnant during anal intercourse if a man's semen comes in contact with a woman's vagina. More important, anal sex puts people at a much higher risk for getting HIV than any other kind of sex. This is because the skin of the rectum can tear during anal intercourse, which then allows easy access for a virus such as HIV to pass from one partner to the other. If a couple decides to have anal sex, they should always use a condom with a water-based lubricant.

TOUGH QUESTIONS

What Is Sexual Harassment?

To harass means "to annoy or disturb someone persistently." To harass someone sexually involves making unwanted sexual remarks, jokes, or gestures. It also involves a person saying something sexual to you or talking about your body in ways that make you feel uncomfortable. Even though it doesn't involve a person actually touching you, it can still be a scary, maddening, and humiliating experience. It is against the law to harass someone sexually. If a person keeps bothering you, whether you're a kid or an adult, then it's important for you to talk to a grown-up you trust about how to stop the harassment.

What Is Sexual Abuse?

Sexual abuse refers to any forced sexual contact or any sexual contact as a result of a threat. Although it is not likely that it will happen to you, sexual abuse can, unfortunately, happen just about anywhere with just about anyone, even in your own home. It can happen between children and adults or children and children, and it often occurs with someone you know, rather than with a stranger, which can make it all the more confusing.

What Is Incest?

Incest is sexual contact or inappropriate physical contact between members of the same family, which includes grandparents or parents, siblings, and uncles, aunts, and cousins.

One terribly confusing thing about sexual abuse, especially incest, is that though the contact is unwanted, it may still arouse feelings of pleasure. This is natural. Human beings respond to pleasurable stimulation. It is the way of the body. Victims of sexual abuse, including incest, may feel confused and bad about this, but they have not done anything wrong. The person who abused them is the one who is wrong.

What Is Rape?

Rape is when one person forces another to have sexual intercourse. A person who is raped needs immediate medical and emotional attention. People who have been raped (it can happen to males as well as females) almost always need someone to talk to about their experience. Fortunately, there are many people out there who can help. For help, call the Childhelp USA toll-free hotline twenty-four hours a day: 1-800-422-4453.

How Do We Protect Ourselves?

If you feel at all funny—suspicious, uncomfortable, mistrustful, scared, weird, spooked, confused—about a person's behavior toward you, verbal (meaning someone talking to you) or physical, tell someone you trust. Remember, you can always talk to a teacher, the school nurse, your doctor, or the police. There are also organizations to call for help.

If you find yourself in a situation where a person tries to talk to you or touch you in a way that feels wrong, it is your absolute right to say, "Stop it!" or "Get away from me!" Even if this person has touched you before, it does not mean that he or she has the right to touch you again. *Please, tell someone right away!* Don't worry or suffer in silence.

What If Sexual Abuse Happens to Me?

The most important thing to do is to get help as soon as possible. Remember, there is nothing you have done to provoke or deserve such painful, hurtful, and unwanted behavior. *It's not your fault,* so don't let feelings of guilt keep you from telling someone right away. Even if you love the person who abused you, you must tell someone, because love or not, this person has done something very wrong. *It's never too late to get help.* Even if you've been afraid to talk about it for a while, there are lots of counselors who are experts in dealing with this and can help you. There are also support groups for people who have gone through this kind of experience. It's very hard to deal with something like sexual abuse if you aren't able to discuss it. Talking with the right person can unburden you and help you recover. Just as a physical wound needs to heal, so does an emotional one.

What Are **STDs?** STD stands for *sexually transmitted disease.* (The term STI, for *sexually transmitted infection,* is frequently used instead of STD.) *Transmitted* means "passed on" or "spread." STDs are diseases that are spread by sexual intercourse and also, in some cases by oral sex or genital contact (which means touching sex organs) with someone who has the disease.

Anyone can get STDs, girl or boy, woman or man. And the fact that there are so many cases of STDs—especially among teenage girls and young women—is one more excellent reason to postpone sex. It's important to know that girls' and women's sexual organs are very sensitive to bacteria and, if exposed, are likely to contract a disease. It's important to know that you don't build up immunity to STDs. In other words, they are not like the measles and chicken pox, which once you've had, you can't get again. With STDs you can be reinfected, and you can reinfect others. Some STDs are caused by bacteria (germs) and are curable with antibiotics.

BACTERIAL STDs   There are several kinds of common bacterial STDs. *Chlamydia* is caused by a bacterium and is the most common STD. One can get chlamydia by having intercourse (vaginal or anal), or through oral sex. Girls and women are at a much higher risk for chlamydia than boys and men. The most common symptom is no symptoms at all, so the disease can be passed from one person to another without either person knowing. One symptom in females can be a yellowish, milky discharge accompanied by burning or itching in the vagina. It's very important to treat chlamydia because it can become chronic (lasting a long time) and may cause *infertility,* which means you can't have children. It can also be passed from mother to child during childbirth.

Gonorrhea is also caused by a bacterium, and sometimes there are no symptoms. One can get gonorrhea through vaginal or anal intercourse, or oral sex. Symptoms in females may include painful urination; greenish, yellowish discharge from either your vagina or urethra (which carries pee out of your body); and itching, burning, or pain around the vagina. If the disease is not treated, it can cause extreme illness, such as heart problems and infertility. It can also be passed from mother to child during childbirth.

the condition and related symptoms, while a cure gets rid of the

Syphilis, a highly contagious bacterial infection, is spread mainly by sexual contact—oral, genital, or anal. The disease can attack a weakened immune system, which means that people with AIDS who indulge in unprotected sexual activity may contract syphilis very easily. The most common symptoms of the STD include one or more chancre sores in the genital area or the mouth, a rash on the soles of the feet or the palms, fatigue, tenderness in the joints, and, occasionally, hair loss. Swollen lymph nodes may also be a symptom, though they also can indicate other problems, such as a strep infection or mumps. Although syphilis can be serious, the good news is that typically it is curable through extensive treatment with strong antibiotics.

VIRAL STDs
Some STDs are caused by viruses. These diseases can be treated but not cured. The difference between a treatment and a cure is that a treatment only helps to lessen

153

the condition and related symptoms, while a cure gets rid of the disease altogether. But remember, you can still get reinfected.

Genital herpes is a virus that affects the area around and in the vagina and around and in the anus. Herpes simplex is a virus that causes a very itchy infection that results in reddish, blisterlike sores in the vaginal or anal area. One can get herpes by sexual intercourse (vaginal or anal), oral sex, or by direct contact with a sore of someone who has the virus. Genital herpes, called herpes 2, is different from herpes 1, which causes blisters or cold sores around the mouth. But herpes 1 can be transferred to the genitals (and vice versa) through oral sex. A doctor can prescribe medicine that will help reduce the pain and itching, and make the sores go away.

Genital warts are caused by a virus called the human papilloma virus that is passed along through sexual intercourse (vaginal or anal), oral sex, or skin-to-skin contact with a person who has the warts. The warts cause itching in the pubic area and around the anus. They may be painless or can be quite painful. The good news if they are painful is that you'll probably get help sooner. Genital warts may be grayish, white, or pinkish in color, and some people think they resemble clusters of miniature cauliflower. Genital warts can always be removed, but they may sometimes recur.

Viral hepatitis (hepatitis B) is the kind of hepatitis that is found in semen, vaginal secretions, and saliva, and it is the only form of hepatitis that is an STD. If not treated, it can be very dangerous, particularly because it affects the liver and can cause permanent damage to that vital organ. Viral hepatitis is extremely contagious. This is one STD that, in addition to being passed on during intercourse, can even be spread

Bugs

Bugs are not considered a serious health risk, but they can be annoying.

PUBIC LICE are tiny bugs that some people think look like crabs. (*Crabs* is a slang term for pubic lice.) Pubic lice love to grow in moist, damp, hairy places. Sound like the pubic area? Sure, and they're passed from partner to partner during sexual contact. Pubic lice can also be spread through sharing sheets, clothing, or towels with someone who has them. Pubic lice cause itchiness in the pubic area. The good news is that the condition is easily cured by applying a prescribed medicine to the pubic area (which will be very itchy) and washing all sheets, towels, and clothes. (Head lice are not pubic lice.)

SCABIES are bugs, a type of mite, that burrow under the skin. It's possible to get scabies without having sexual contact. As with pubic lice, you can get them by sharing sheets and towels with someone who has them. The number-one symptom of scabies is severe itching, particularly in the genital area but also in other parts of the body, except for the head and neck. Using the proper medication and washing all clothes, sheets, and towels will get rid of them.

from an infected person to an uninfected person by kissing. Often the disease has no symptoms and can be passed from one person to another without anyone knowing. It can also be passed from mother to child during childbirth.

The good news is that there's a new vaccine for hepatitis B

Piercing, Tattooing, and Hepatitis B

If you are younger than eighteen and you want to get your ears (or other parts of your body) pierced, you'll need a parent or guardian to accompany you and sign a permission form. It's important that you go to a trusted professional who always uses brand-new needles. The use of an unclean needle in a procedure even as simple as ear piercing can pass on hepatitis. If you're considering getting a tattoo, you'll need to wait until you're eighteen. And again, always see a trustworthy professional.

that works extremely well and is recommended by pediatricians for young children. If you haven't had this vaccine, talk to your parents or doctor about it.

HIV AND AIDS   Your immune system is what protects you against any infection or allergic disease that might be attacking your body. It's your first line of defense. This is why a healthy immune system is so important to your health.

HIV stands for *human immunodeficiency virus*. The virus attacks the human immune system, making it difficult to fight off infections and diseases. HIV is the virus that causes the disease AIDS. AIDS stands for *acquired immune deficiency syndrome,* and it is the last stage of HIV.

People are said to have AIDS when the virus has finally attacked the immune system so severely that the body is no longer able to defend itself against illnesses. These infections, which come more and more often and last longer and longer, destroy the body's ability to fight back. Eventually one of these numerous infections will cause death.

Bleak as this sounds, the treatments for HIV and AIDS are increasingly effective. And people are living longer and longer with HIV before developing AIDS. Unfortunately, there are still many myths about HIV and AIDS. But you *can't* get HIV by limited physical contact such as:

❖ being near someone with the virus or AIDS
❖ using the same toilet seat
❖ drinking out of the same glass
❖ holding hands
❖ hugging or kissing

How Can I Get HIV?

You *can* get HIV from an infected person through:

- sexual intercourse (anal or vaginal) or oral sex
- sharing needles (when shooting up drugs)

What Does the Term *Practicing Abstinence* Mean?

The only way to totally protect yourself from getting HIV and other STDs, or from becoming pregnant, is by not having sex. This is called *practicing abstinence*. Because STDs can be spread in more than one way, practicing abstinence nowadays means not having oral sex, or vaginal or anal intercourse.

What Does the Term *Safer Sex* Mean?

Please remember, it's important for everyone who decides to have sex to protect themselves. And there's a lot a person *can and must do* to be protected. This is called practicing *safer sex*. To help avoid STDs and pregnancy, the most important thing to know is that you must use high-quality condoms *each and every time you have sex*.

THE ABC's OF BIRTH CONTROL

What Is Birth Control?

Birth control is the method people use to prevent pregnancy.

What Are Contraceptives?

Contraceptives are forms of birth control such as the condom and the pill.

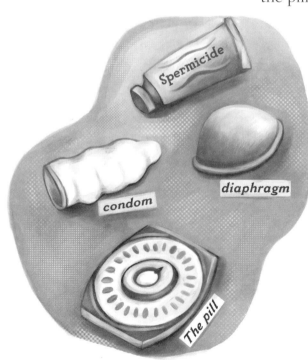

159

CONDOMS, CONDOMS, CONDOMS

When used with a spermicide, latex condoms are the best protection against HIV and other STDs and unwanted pregnancy. It is very important to remember that a condom can be used only once.

Male Latex Condoms

The latex sheath fits very snugly around the penis and often has what's called a reservoir at the end, where the semen collects after ejaculation. Latex is a strong, nonporous material. (Nonporous means having no pores, or tiny holes.) This means it protects against pregnancy and also protects both the vagina and the penis from bacteria and viruses in semen and vaginal secretions, which may carry infections.

Natural Skin Condoms

These do not offer adequate protection against infections. They are not as strong as latex condoms and can easily develop tiny holes or tears. They also have pores, which may allow viruses or bacteria to get through.

Female Polyurethane Condoms

This type of condom is worn by the woman in her vagina. It is effective in preventing pregnancies and STDs. No prescription is required and it can be purchased in a drugstore. Like the male latex condom, it can be worn only once, and a new condom must be used each and every time sex occurs.

What Everyone Should Know about Male Condoms

In order to be effective, a condom must be used each and every time a person has sex. When used with a spermicide, condoms are 97 percent effective against pregnancy. Keep in mind these general parameters for male condoms:

- They must be made of latex or polyurethane.
- They should never be used with oil-based products such as Vaseline or skin lotions, as these can destroy their effectiveness.
- They should be used with a water-based lubricant (both inside and outside of the condom), which can be bought in a drugstore.
- Only one condom should be worn at a time. Putting on two condoms, one on top of the other, does not provide more protection and can cause the condoms to rip. This is because the two layers of material rub against each other, causing friction that may tear one or both condoms. Also, a man should not wear a condom if the woman is wearing a female condom (and vice versa).
- Condoms have expiration dates and should not be used beyond the date indicated.
- Condoms should be kept in cool dark places, such as drawers, and not in wallets or anywhere they'll be exposed to heat or sunlight.
- Condoms are not expensive. You don't need a prescription to buy them, and they can be purchased over the counter in a drugstore, even by teenagers.

Hormonal Methods of Birth Control

The *birth control pill* is a *hormonal* form of contraception. That means it prevents ovulation by changing the level of the female hormones so that the woman's egg is not released. As we know, without the egg, there can be no pregnancy. The pill also makes the lining of the uterus thinner, which makes it harder for the egg to implant, and if a fertilized egg cannot settle into the lining and get nutrients, there can be no pregnancy. The birth control pill must be taken daily. Missing even one pill can cause a woman to become pregnant if she has intercourse. The pills may be purchased at a drugstore but are available only with a prescription. Birth control pills are 92–99 percent effective in preventing pregnancy. Birth control pills do not protect against STDs so condoms with spermicide are still recommended in addition to the pill. There are other effective methods of hormonal birth control, such as Depo-Provera and the vaginal ring.

Birth Control Champion

We can't talk about birth control without paying tribute to Margaret Sanger, a devoted nurse. More than eighty years ago, she saw numerous poor women die from having too many children. It was against the law at that time to distribute birth control materials or even to publish information about it, but Sanger was determined to change the laws, even if it meant she had to spend time in jail, which she did. She believed women would never have control over their health and their lives until they were able to plan, as well as to prevent, pregnancy. In 1916 she opened the first family planning clinic in the United States. Margaret Sanger was the founder of what is now called Planned Parenthood.

Other Methods of Birth Control

THE DIAPHRAGM   The *diaphragm* is round and rubbery and shaped like a shallow bowl. It must be used with spermicidal jelly or cream in order to be effective. The diaphragm is flexible and made to be folded so that it can be inserted into the vagina, high enough to cover the cervix. There it prevents sperm from entering the uterus. Diaphragms come in different sizes and must be fitted by a doctor or nurse. A diaphragm can be purchased only with a prescription.

FOAMS, SPRAYS, AND FILM   These do not require prescriptions and can be bought over the counter. They are inserted into the vagina fifteen minutes before a couple has intercourse. *Used alone, they are not very effective forms of birth control.*

Emergency Contraception, or EC, prevents pregnancy from occurring after unprotected sex. Unprotected sex might occur because a woman forgot to take her birth control pill, or because her partner's condom broke, or because she was forced to have unprotected sex.

EC is a high dose of birth control pills or progestin-only pills. It's effective when taken within five days of unprotected sex—but the sooner it's taken, the more effective it is. EC prevents pregnancy by stopping ovulation, fertilization, or implantation.

A doctor or clinician usually prescribes EC, but in some states a pharmacy can participate in the EC Pharmacy Program, which makes it possible for a patient to get EC without having to see a doctor first. EC does not offer protection from STDs or HIV/AIDS.

When You Have Questions about Sex

Talk to your parents, aunt, uncle, or other trusted adults about their views on sex. See if they can answer your questions.

Libraries and bookstores are also great sources of information. There are a number of wonderful books about puberty and sex written for preteens and teens. (For some of our suggestions, see "Recommended Reading," which begins on page 172.) There are also hotlines you can call to get your questions answered. (See the listings that begin on page 168.) These calls are considered to be confidential, which means nobody will ask for your name and the calls will not appear on your phone bill.

Can Couples Be Close and Loving Without Having Sex?

You bet. People discover their own ways, but here are some ideas:

- holding hands
- going for long walks together
- going on picnics
- dancing wherever you can
- listening to music together
- talking, talking, talking!

What If I Want to Hug and Kiss But Not Have Sex?

It's a wonderful feeling to hug and kiss a person you love. The best news of all—and there's a lot of good news about puberty—is that you can hug and kiss the person you love all you want without having to move on to the risky business of intercourse. However, it's important for a couple to discuss exactly how far they are willing to go *before they start kissing*.

Don't Rush

Sex is not something that is meant to be rushed through or gotten over with. There's plenty of time. Puberty is a good time to dream about the future. It's a good time to explore the subjects that interest you. It's a good time to find out about yourself and the world around you.

What to Do in the Afternoon

Lots of kids don't know what to do after school if they are not involved with sports or other extra-curricular activities. These are the hours when some kids make the wrong choices—from having unprotected sex to taking drugs. If your school doesn't offer afternoon sports or other programs or clubs, spend time at your local library—it's free. Also, talk to your parents and teachers about starting an after-school program.

Many Rivers to Cross

*L*ife is full of passages, and puberty is one of the most important ones. These passages are filled with exciting and illuminating learning experiences, but not every single one is fun. We know you know this already.

Always remember, although you are unique and there is nobody like you, everybody, *but everybody,* who is about your age is going through what you're going through. Believe it or not, they've all had their bad days. Not only that, but every adult—from your favorite rock star to your parents—has gone through puberty, too. They've all had their share of embarrassing experiences, cringe words, and cringe *moments.* You are not alone.

There are so many rivers to cross in life. But don't forget there are bridges across them. These bridges include friends, moms, pops, sisters, brothers, grandparents, uncles and aunts, teachers, coaches, school nurses, doctors, ministers, therapists—even your pets. Thank goodness for bridges, and here's to a safe and healthy crossing.

Resources for Preteens and Teens

Toll-free Hotlines

Child Abuse Hotline
Hours: 24 hours daily
1-800-422-4453 (1-800-4-A-CHILD) (United States and Canada)

Covenant House Nineline
Hours: 24 hours daily
1-800-999-9999; 1-800-999-9915 (TTY/TDD for the hearing impaired)
www.covenanthouse.org; www.nineline.org
Provides crisis intervention and referrals to callers younger than twenty-one and their families. Young people call about various personal issues, including family matters, relationship problems, child abuse, family violence, homelessness, running away, substance abuse, and gang involvement.

Girls and Boys Town, National Hotline
Hours: 24 hours daily
1-800-448-3000; 1-800-448-1833 (TTY for the hearing impaired)
www.girlsandboystown.org/hotline
A crisis resource and referral line for teens and parents.

National Runaway Switchboard

Hours: 24 hours daily

1-800-621-4000 (United States only); 1-800-621-0394 (TDD for the
hearing impaired)

www.nrscrisisline.org

A not-for-profit volunteer organization whose mission is to provide crisis intervention and referrals for youth through national and local telephone switchboards, as
well as advocacy and educational services pertaining to the problems of youth.

The Trevor Project

Hours: 24 hours daily

1-866-488-7386

www.thetrevorproject.org

A nonprofit endeavor to promote acceptance of gay and questioning teenagers
and to aid in suicide prevention for those among that group. Maintains a free
suicide-prevention line.

Helpful Organizations

Girls Incorporated, National Headquarters

120 Wall Street, 3rd Floor

New York, New York 10005-3902

212-509-2000

www.girlsinc.org

Girls Incorporated, National Resource Center

441 W. Michigan Street

Indianapolis, Indiana 46202-3233

317-634-7546

A national organization that provides various programs for girls ages six to eighteen,
including Preventing Adolescent Pregnancy, an age-phased program for girls ages
nine to eighteen that pertains to health and sexuality education, assertiveness,
pregnancy/STD/HIV prevention, and parent/girl communication skills.

169

Go Ask Alice

www.goaskalice.columbia.edu

Columbia University's health question-and-answer Internet site.

IMPACT

1-800-345-5425

www.prepareinc.com

With chapters throughout the United States, provides self-defense training for women, teens, and younger kids.

Mind on the Media

www.motm.org

A nonprofit organization dedicated to raising public awareness about the negative effects of images in the media.

National Youth Advocacy Coalition (NYAC)

1638 R Street NW, Suite 300

Washington, D.C. 20009

202-319-7596; 1-800-541-9622; 202-319-9513 (TTY for the hearing impaired)

www.nyacyouth.org/youth_connections.html

Focuses solely on improving the lives of gay, lesbian, bisexual, and transgender (GLBT) youth through advocacy, education, and dissemination of information. The Bridges Project provides information, referrals, and materials to GLBT youth, the agencies that serve them, educators, health-care professionals, and other supportive adults.

Parents, Families, and Friends of Lesbians and Gays (PFLAG), National Office

1726 M Street NW, Suite 400

Washington, D.C. 20036

202-467-8180

www.pflag.org

A national organization that promotes the health and well-being of gay, lesbian, bisexual, and transgender persons, their families, and friends through support, education, and advocacy. Serving more than 77,000 members and supporters, with affiliates located in more than 425 communities throughout the United States.

Planned Parenthood Federation of America, Inc.
810 Seventh Avenue
New York, New York 10019
212-514-7800; 1-800-230-7526 (1-800-230-PLAN)
A national family-planning organization that provides comprehensive reproductive and primary health-care services as well as educational programs for youths and their parents. Call 1-800-230-PLAN for the Planned Parenthood center nearest you.

A great alternative reading resource for girls and parents alike:

New Moon Magazine
www.newmoon.org
An award-winning and forward-thinking magazine for girls ages eight to fourteen. The magazine features fiction, poetry, artwork, science experiments, and articles about the lives of girls and women around the world. It's also an excellent tool for teachers, homeschoolers, and girls' group leaders.

Recommended Reading

Suggested Reading for Teens and Parents

Abner, Allison, and Linda Villarosa. *Finding Our Way: The Teen Girls' Survival Guide.* New York: HarperCollins, 1995.

Bass, Ellen, and Kate Kaufman. *Free Your Mind: The Book for Gay, Lesbian, and Bisexual Youth—and Their Allies.* New York: HarperCollins, 1996.

Bell, Ruth. *Changing Bodies, Changing Lives: A Book for Teens on Sex and Relationships.* New York: Vintage Books, 1988.

Bolden, Tonya. *Body Outlaws: Young Women Write About Body Image and Identity.* Edited by Ophira Edut. Seattle: Seal Press, 2000.

Bolden, Tonya, ed. *33 Things Every Girl Should Know: Stories, Songs, Poems, and Smart Talk by 33 Extraordinary Women.* New York: Crown Publishers, 1998.

Criswell, Patti Kelley. *A Smart Girl's Guide to Friendship Troubles.* Wisconsin: American Girl, 2003.

Gardner-Loulan, JoAnn, Bonnie Lopez, and Marcia Quackenbush. *Period: A Girl's Guide to Menstruation.* 4th ed. Minnesota: Book Peddlers, 2001.

Harris, Robie H. *It's Perfectly Normal: A Book about Changing Bodies, Growing Up, Sex, and Sexual Health.* 10th anniv. ed. Boston: Candlewick Press, 2004.

Huegel, Kelly. *GBLTQ: The Survival Guide for Queer and Questioning Teens.* Minneapolis: Free Spirit Publishing, 2003.

Madaras, Lynda, and Area Madaras. *My Body, My Self for Girls: A "What's Happening to My Body?" Quizbook and Journal.* 2d ed. Newmarket Press, 2000.

——*My Feelings, My Self.* New York: Newmarket Press, 1993

——*The What's Happening to My Body? Book for Girls: A Growing Up Guide for Parents and Daughters.* 3d ed. New York: Newmarket Press 2000.

Marcus, Eric. *Is It a Choice? Answers to 300 of the Most Frequently Asked Questions about Gays and Lesbians.* San Francisco: HarperSanFrancisco, 1993.

Schafer, Lee Valorie. *The Care and Keeping of You: The Body Book for Girls.* Wisconsin: Pleasant Company Publications, 1998.

Suggested Fiction for Teens

Anderson, Laurie Halse. *Speak.* New York: Farrar, Straus and Giroux, 1999.

Bauer, Joan. *Hope Was Here.* New York: G. P. Putnam's Sons, 2000.

Bauer, Marion Dane, ed. *Am I Blue? Coming Out from the Silence.* New York: HarperCollins, 1994.

Blume, Judy. *Are You There, God? It's Me, Margaret.* New York: Bradbury Press, 1970.

Carlson, Lori, ed. *Cool Salsa: Bilingual Poems on Growing Up Latino in the United States.* New York: Henry Holt & Company, 1994.

Choi, Sook Nyul. *Year of Impossible Goodbyes.* Boston: Houghton Mifflin Company, 1991.

Cisneros, Sandra. *The House on Mango Street.* Houston: Arte Publico Press, 1983.

Cofer, Judith Ortiz. *An Island Like You: Stories of the Barrio.* New York: Orchard Books, 1995.

Creech, Sharon. *Bloomability.* New York: HarperCollins, 1998.

Dorris, Michael. *Morning Girl.* New York: Hyperion, 1992.

Flake, Sharon G. *The Skin I'm In.* New York: Hyperion, 1998.

Forbes, Kathryn. *Mama's Bank Account.* San Diego, Calif.: Harcourt, Inc., 1968.

Frank, Anne. *The Diary of a Young Girl.* New York: Doubleday, 1995.

Guy, Rosa. *The Friends.* New York: Bantam Books, 1991.

Hazen, Lynn E. *Mermaid Mary Margaret.* New York: Bloomsbury Children's Books, 2004.

Hewett, Lorri. *Dancer.* New York: Dutton Children's Books, 1999.

McKay, Hilary. *Saffy's Angel.* New York: Margaret K. McElderry Books, 2002.

173

Nye, Naomi Shihab. *Habibi*. New York: Simon Pulse, 1999.

Ryan, Pam Muñoz. *Esperanza Rising*. New York: Scholastic Press, 2000.

Sinclair, April. *Coffee Will Make You Black*. New York: Avon Books, 1995.

Smith, Betty. *A Tree Grows in Brooklyn*. New York: Perennial Classics, 1998.

Staples, Suzanne F. *Shabanu: Daughter of the Wind*. New York: Alfred A. Knopf, 1989.

Wiles, Deborah. *Each Little Bird That Sings*. New York: Harcourt, Inc., 2005.

Yep, Laurence. *Child of the Owl*. New York: HarperTrophy, 1990.

Suggested Reading for Parents

Brumberg, Joan Jacobs. *The Body Project: An Intimate History of American Girls*. New York: Vintage Books, 1998.

Faber, Adele, and Elaine Mazlish. *How to Talk So Kids Will Listen & Listen So Kids Will Talk*. New York: HarperResource, 2005.

Orenstein, Peggy. *Schoolgirls: Young Women, Self-Esteem, and the Confidence Gap*. New York: Doubleday, 1994.

Pipher, Mary. *Reviving Ophelia: Saving the Selves of Adolescent Girls*. New York: Ballantine Books, 1995.

Ponton, Lynn. *The Romance of Risk: Why Teenagers Do the Things They Do*. New York: BasicBooks, 1997.

Simmons, Rachel. *Odd Girl Out: The Hidden Culture of Aggression in Girls*. New York: Harcourt, Inc., 2002.

Wiseman, Rosalind. *Queen Bees and Wannabees: Helping Your Daughter Survive Cliques, Boyfriends, and Other Realities of Adolescence*. New York: Three Rivers Press, 2002.

Wolf, Anthony E. *Get Out of My Life, but First Could You Drive Me and Cheryl to the Mall? A Parent's Guide to the New Teenager*. New York: Noonday Press, 1991.

Index

acne, 38–57
  causes of, 39–42, 54
  concealing pimples, 50–52
  controlling, 42–46, 49–50
  diet and, 41–42
  feelings about, 38, 52–57
  medications, 43, 47, 48, 49–50
acupressure, 111
acupuncture, 110–111
AIDS (acquired immunodeficiency syndrome), 153, 157–58
alternative medicine, 110–117
amenorrhea, 27, 82
anal sex, 134, 149, 152, 153, 154, 158
anorexia nervosa, 26–27, 27*
antibiotics, 49, 64, 152, 153
  yeast infections and, 64
antiperspirant, 22
appearance
  comfort with, 24, 25, 51, 56–57

Page numbers set in italic refer to illustrations.

cultural messages about, 16, 24, 25, 26, 30, 31, 32
  worries about, 29–31, 53–54
aromatherapy, 116–117

benzoyl peroxide, 43, 47, 49–50
bingeing, 27, 28
birth control, 159–63
  birth control pills, 159, *159*, 162
  condoms, 149, 158, 159, *159*, 160–61
  diaphragm, *159*, 163
bisexuality, 142, 143
blackheads, 39, 40
bladder infections, 80–81
bloodstains, removing, 73
body
  changes in, 5–7, 10–12, 15–16, 21, 23–24, *24*, 39, 60, 67
  feelings about, 24, 25, 87
body hair, *16*, 16–20
body image. *See* appearance